EASY PIANO

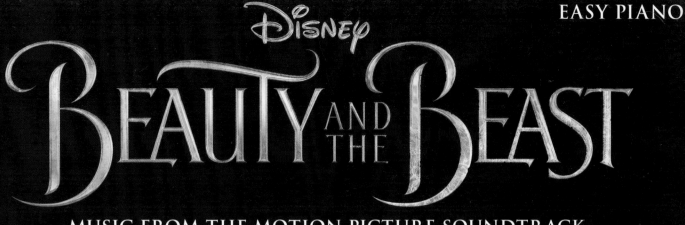

Disney
BEAUTY AND THE BEAST

MUSIC FROM THE MOTION PICTURE SOUNDTRACK

Music by ALAN MENKEN
Lyrics by HOWARD ASHMAN and TIM RICE

ISBN 978-1-4950-9457-6

Motion Picture Artwork,TM & Copyright
© 2017 Disney Enterprises, Inc.

Wonderland Music Company, Inc.
Walt Disney Music Company

DISTRIBUTED BY

7777 W. BLUEMOUND RD. P.O. BOX 13819 MILWAUKEE, WI 53213

In Australia Contact:
Hal Leonard Australia Pty. Ltd.
4 Lentara Court
Cheltenham, Victoria, 3192 Australia
Email: ausadmin@halleonard.com.au

Visit Hal Leonard Online at
www.halleonard.com

ARIA

Music by ALAN MENKEN
Lyrics by TIM RICE

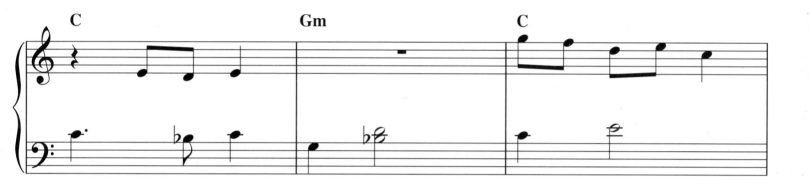

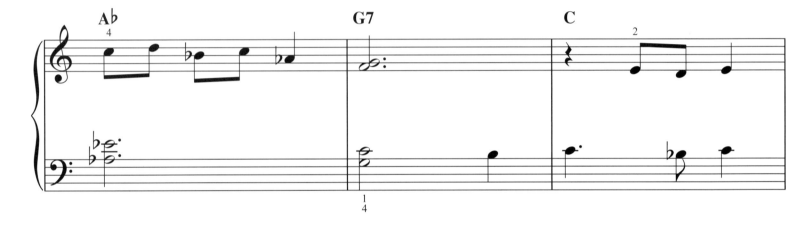

Oh, how di -

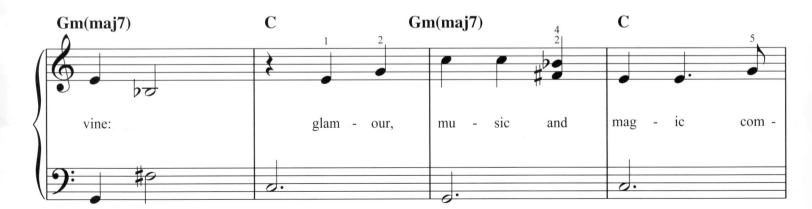

vine: glam - our,   mu - sic and   mag - ic com -

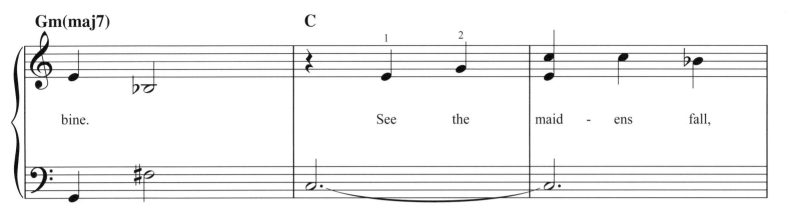

bine.   See   the   maid - ens   fall,

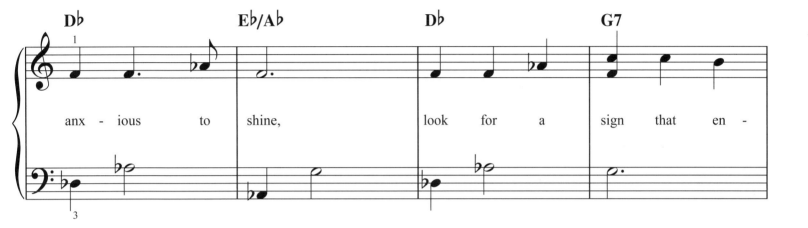

anx - ious   to   shine,   look   for   a   sign   that   en -

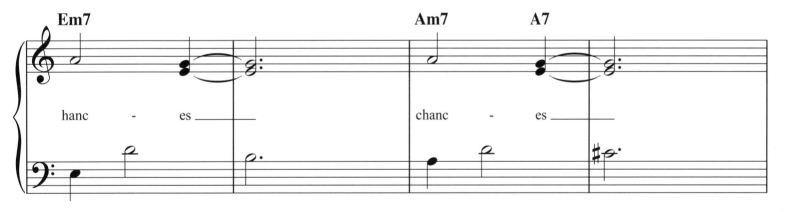

hanc - es _____   chanc - es _____

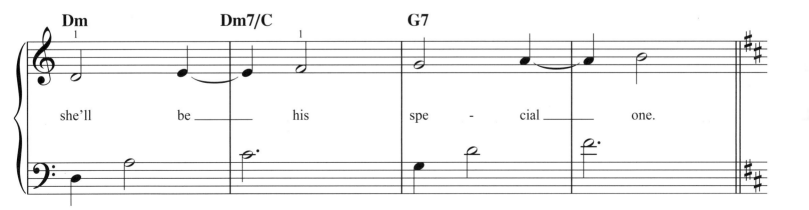

she'll   be ___   his   spe - cial ___   one.

Fast

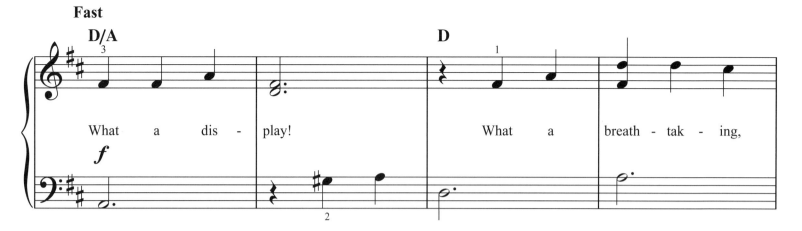

What a dis - play!   What a breath - tak - ing,

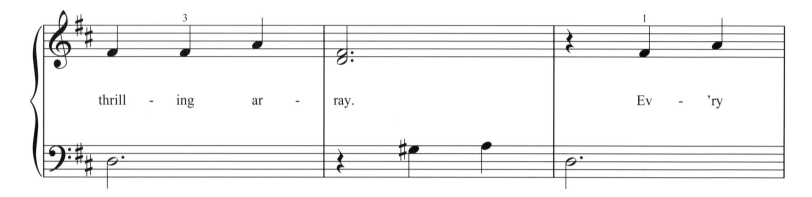

thrill - ing ar - ray.   Ev - 'ry

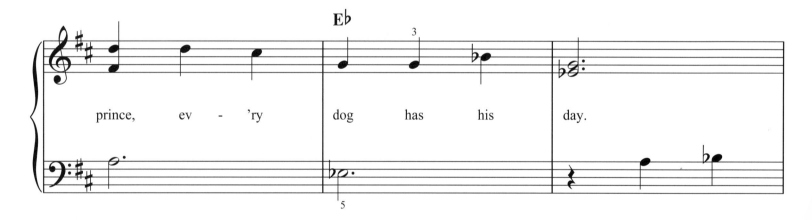

prince, ev - 'ry dog has his day.

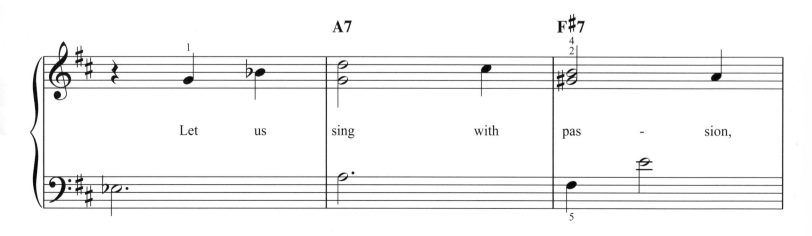

Let us sing with pas - sion,

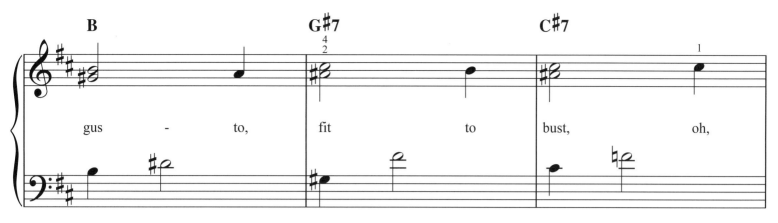

gus - to, fit to bust, oh,

not a care in the world.

BELLE

Music by ALAN MENKEN
Lyrics by HOWARD ASHMAN

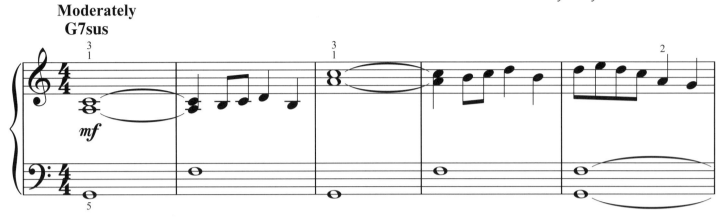

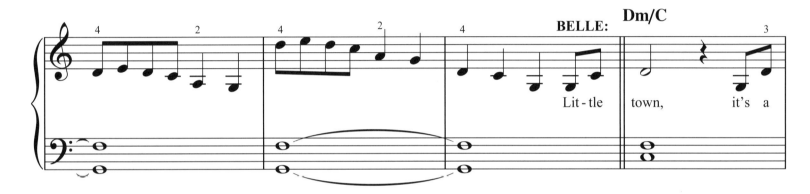

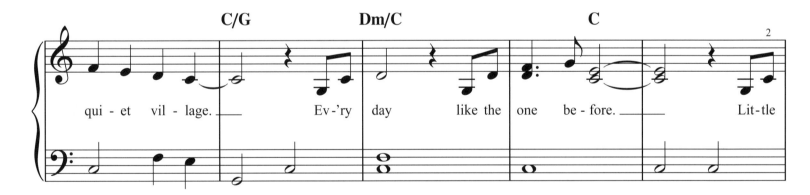

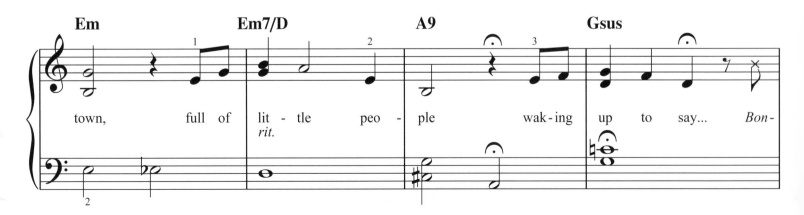

Moderately fast, in 2

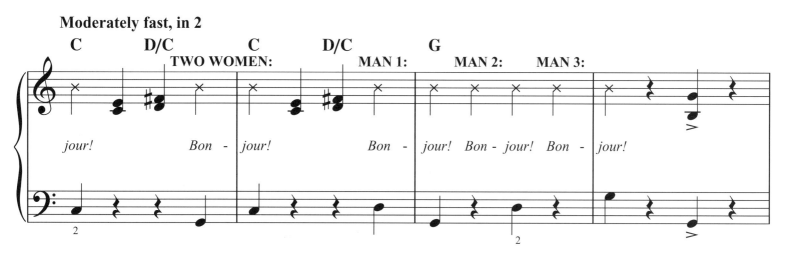

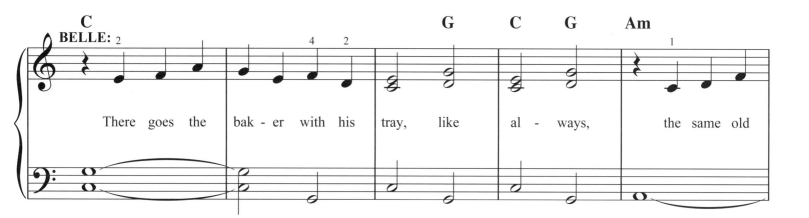

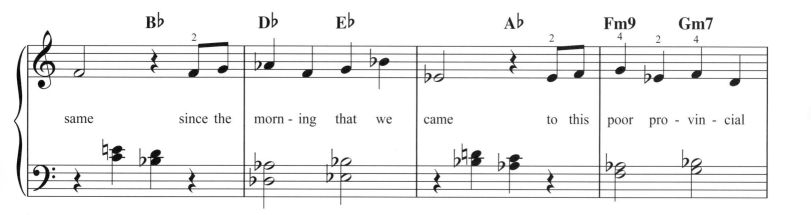

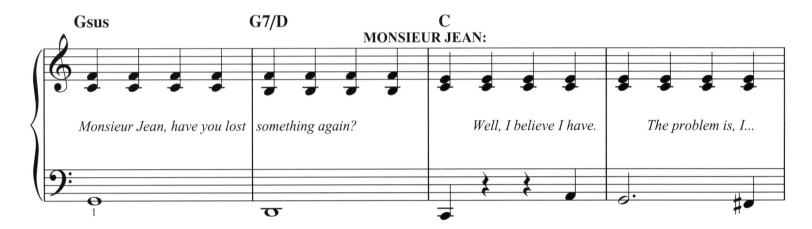

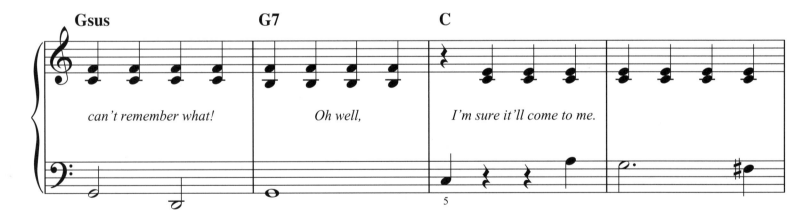

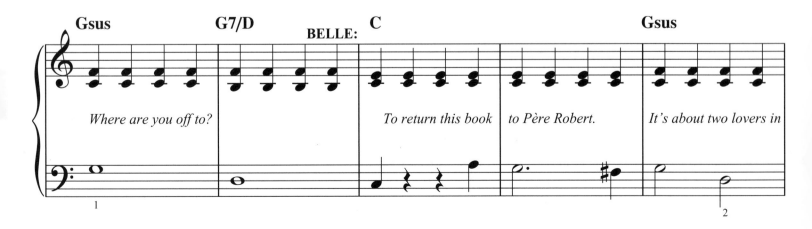

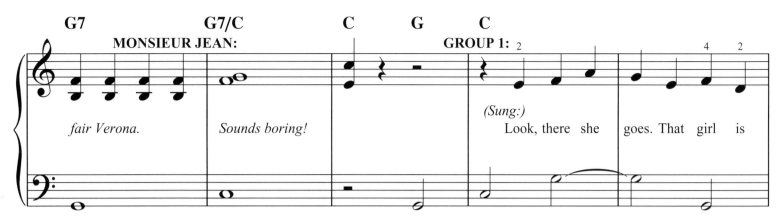

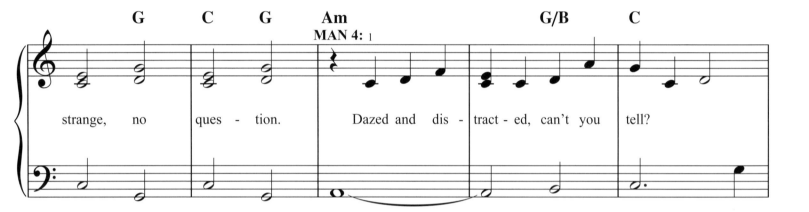

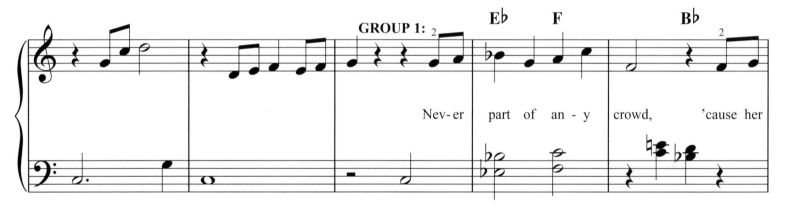

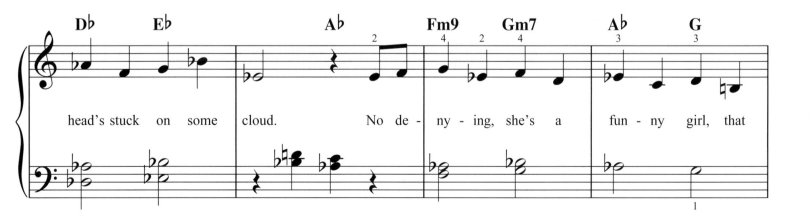

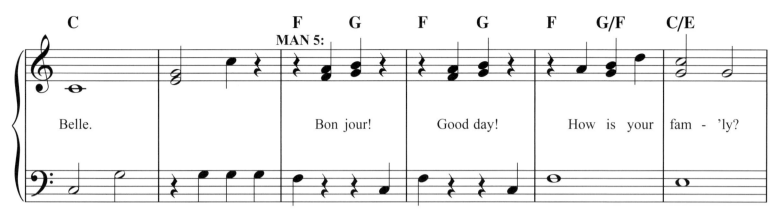

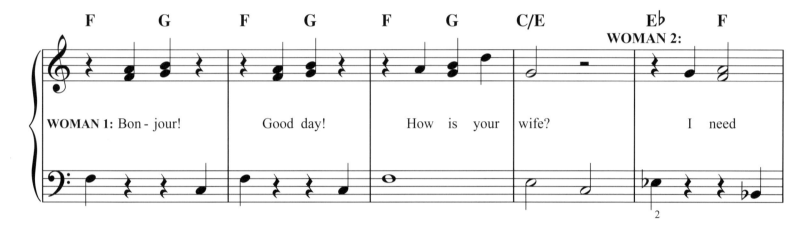

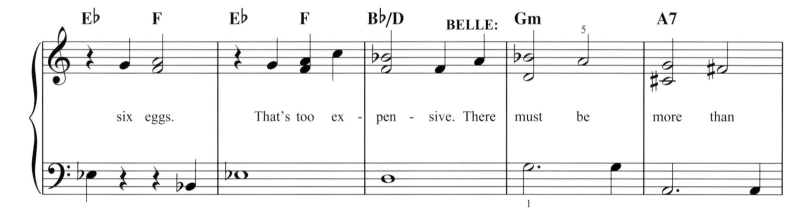

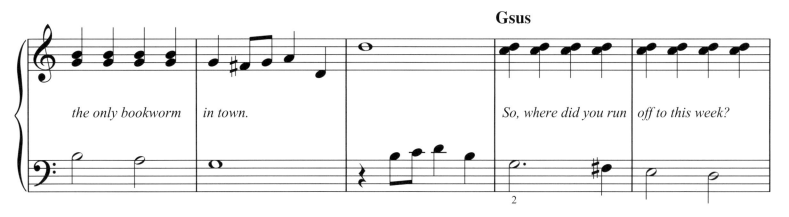

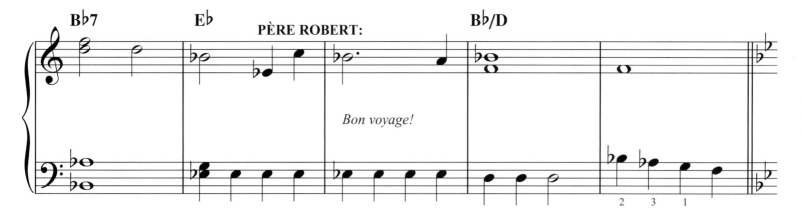

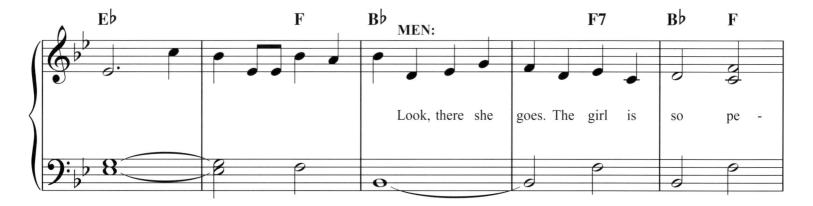

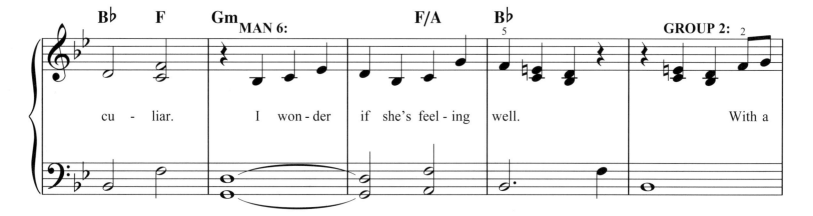

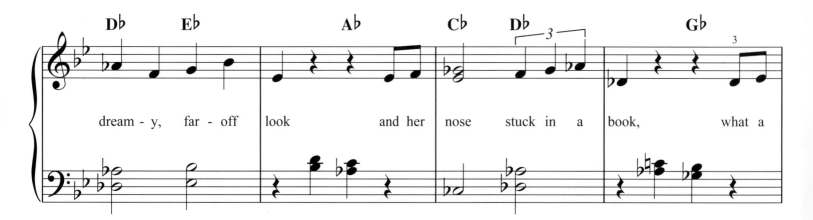

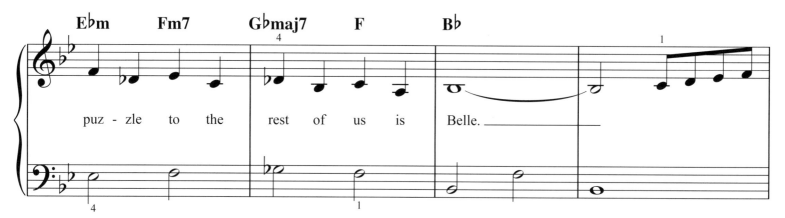

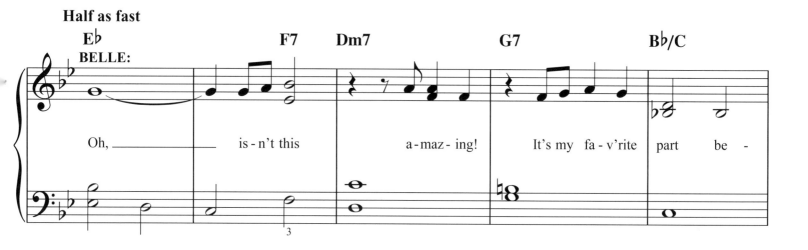

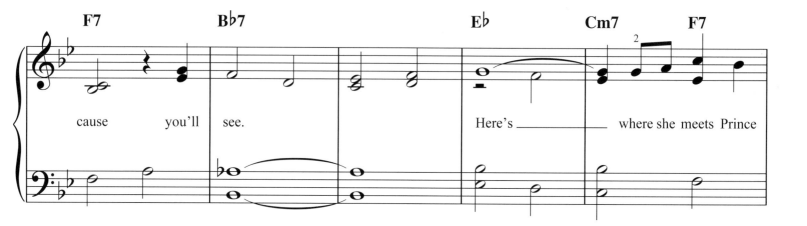

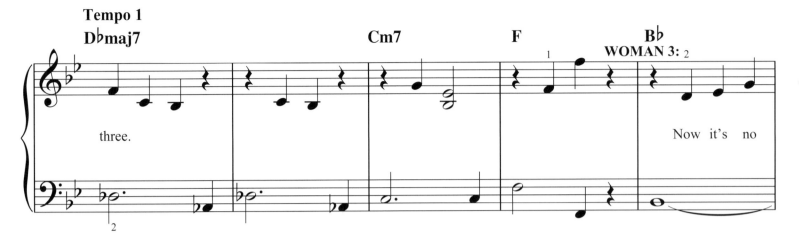

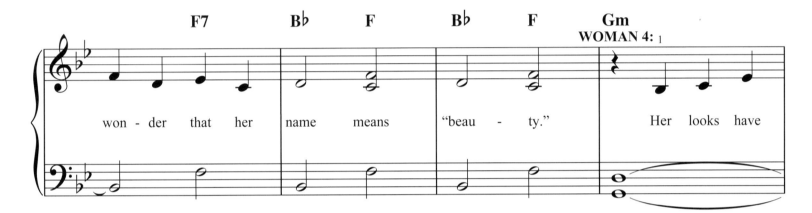

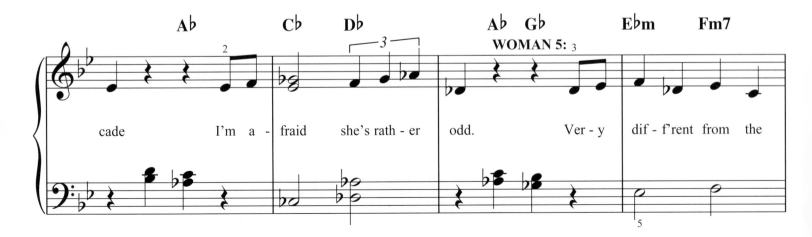

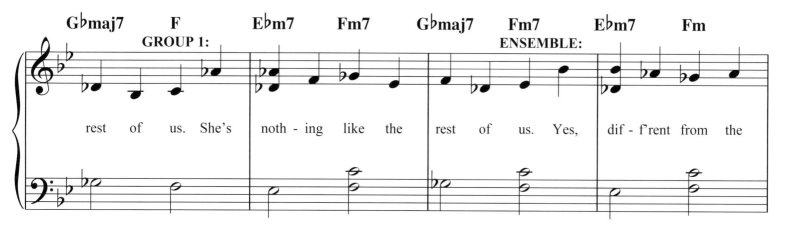

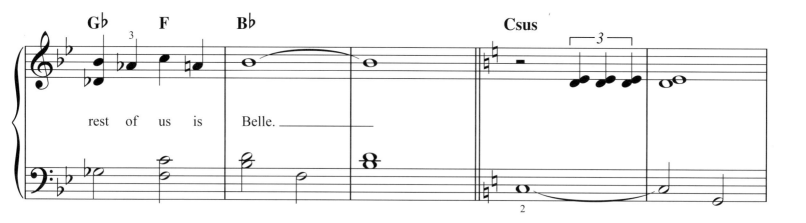

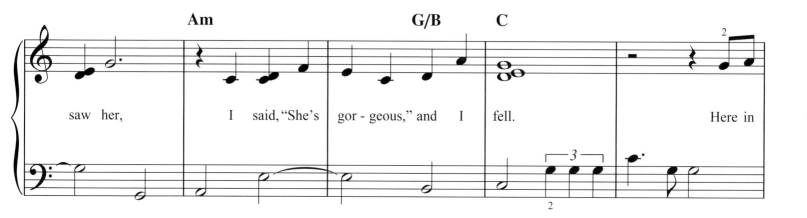

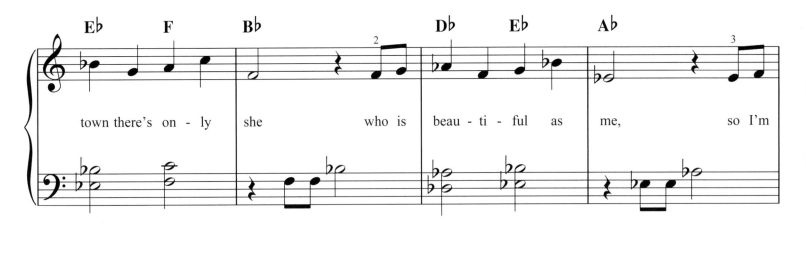

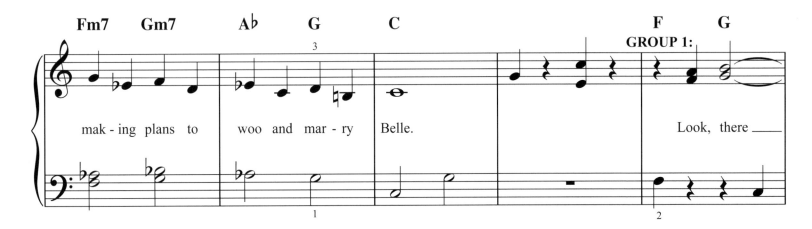

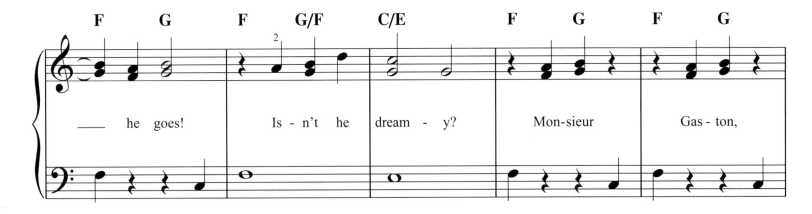

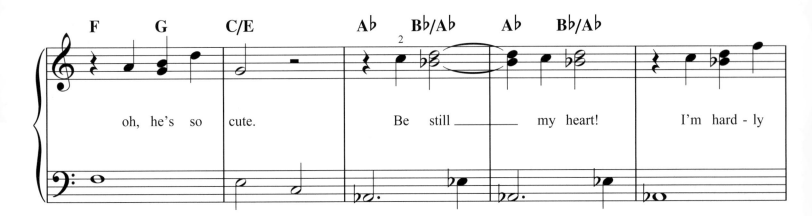

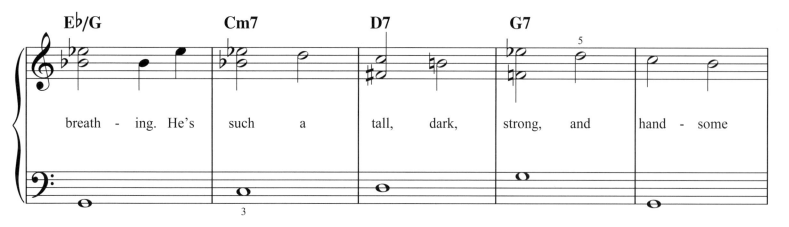

breath - ing. He's such a tall, dark, strong, and hand - some

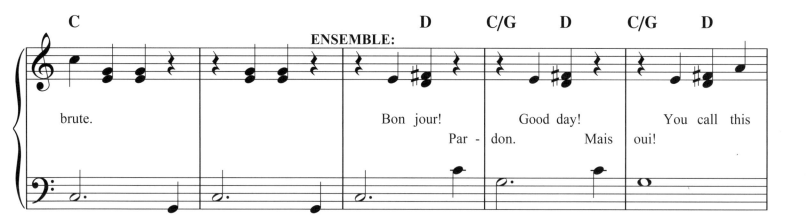

ENSEMBLE:

brute. Bon jour! Good day! You call this
Par - don. Mais oui!

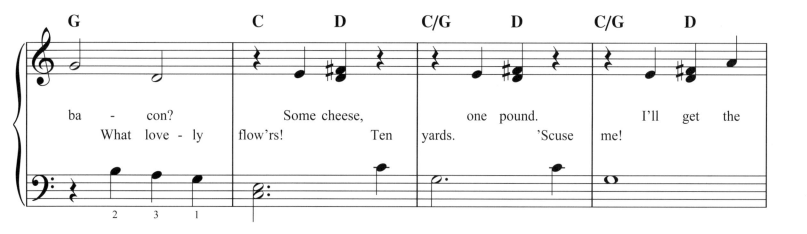

ba - con? Some cheese, one pound. I'll get the
What love - ly flow'rs! Ten yards. 'Scuse me!

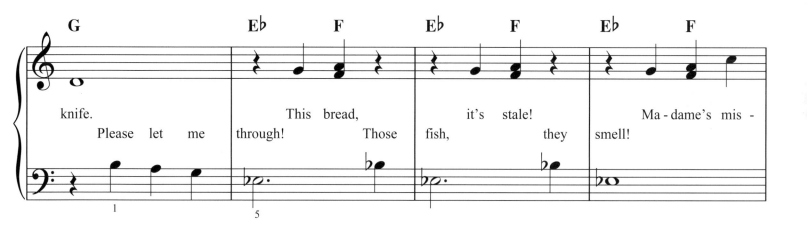

knife. This bread, it's stale! Ma - dame's mis -
Please let me through! Those fish, they smell!

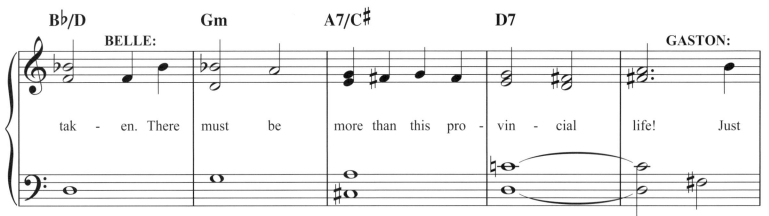

BELLE:

tak - en. There must be more than this pro - vin - cial life! Just

GASTON:

watch! I'm go - ing to make Belle my wife.

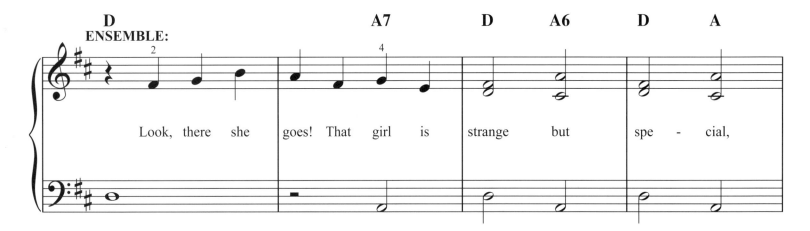

ENSEMBLE:

Look, there she goes! That girl is strange but spe - cial,

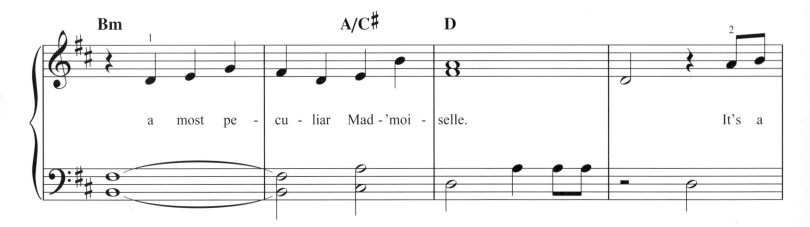

a most pe - cu - liar Mad -'moi - selle. It's a

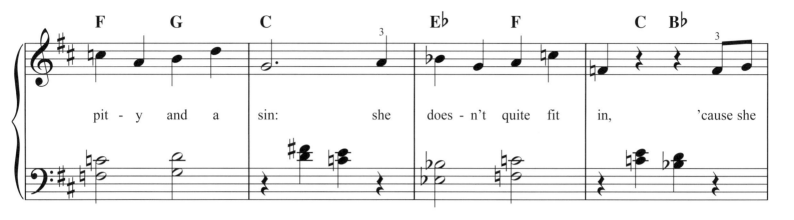

pit - y and a sin: she does - n't quite fit in, 'cause she

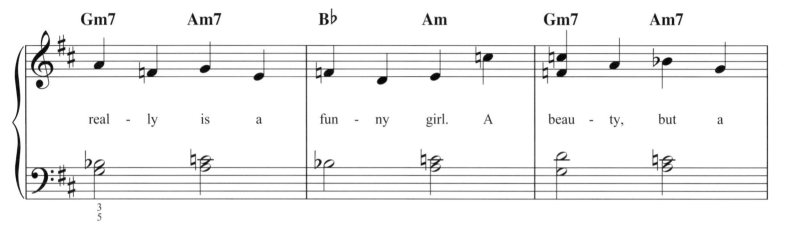

real - ly is a fun - ny girl. A beau - ty, but a

fun - ny girl. She real - ly is a fun - ny girl, _____

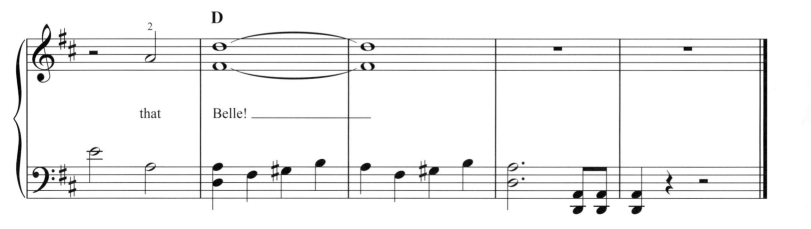

that Belle! _____

GASTON

Music by ALAN MENKEN
Lyrics by HOWARD ASHMAN
(Contains previously unreleased
lyrics by Howard Ashman)

Moderately fast Waltz

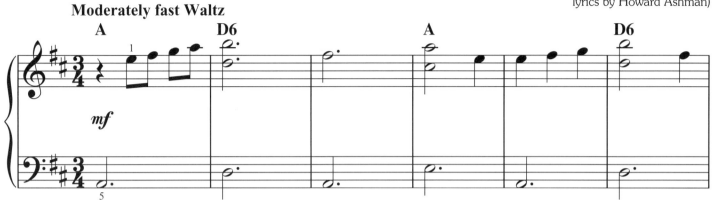

LeFOU:
Gosh, it dis - turbs me to see you, Gas - ton,

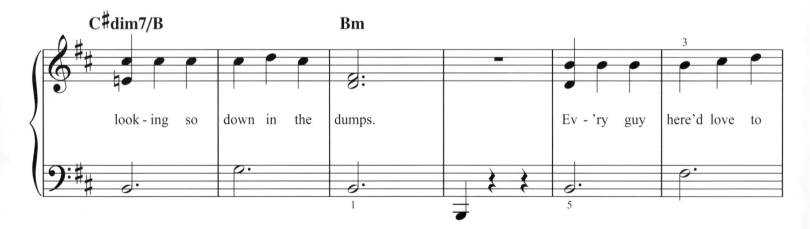

look - ing so down in the dumps. Ev - 'ry guy here'd love to

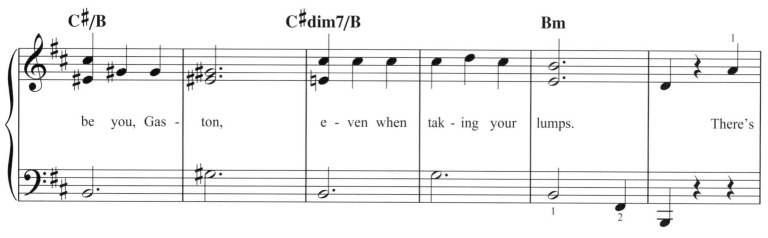

be you, Gas - ton, e - ven when tak - ing your lumps. There's

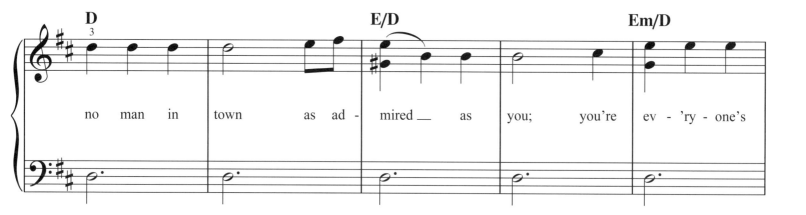

no man in town as ad - mired ___ as you; you're ev - 'ry - one's

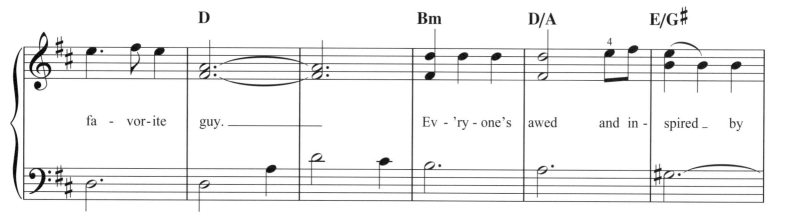

fa - vor-ite guy. _____ Ev - 'ry-one's awed and in - spired _ by

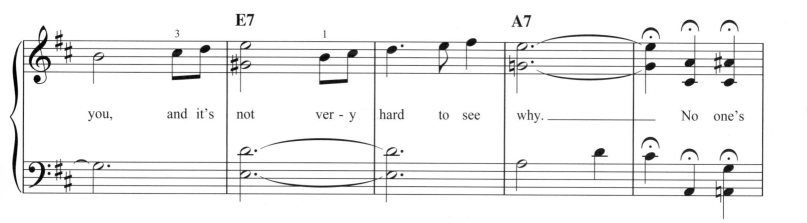

you, and it's not ver - y hard to see why. _____ No one's

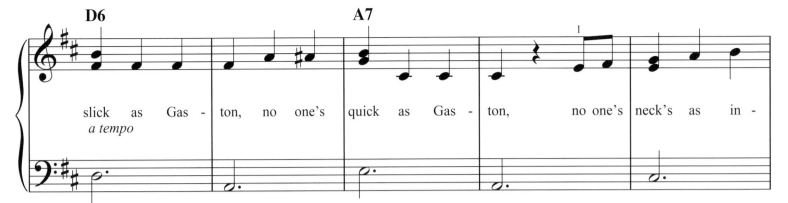

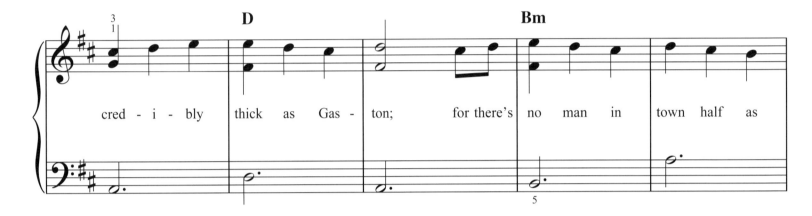

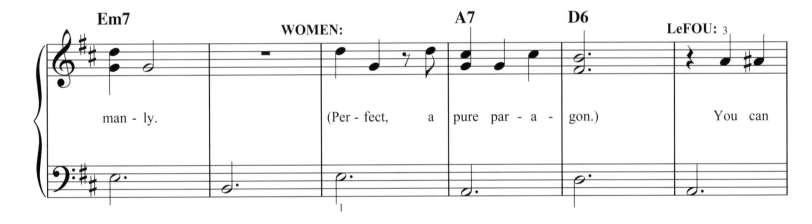

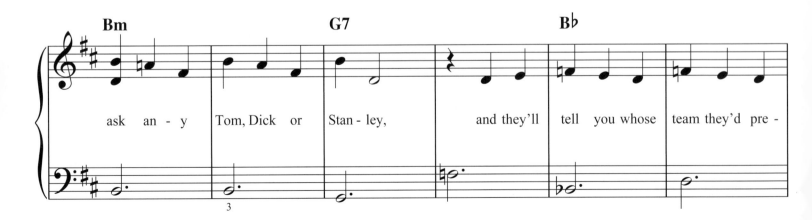

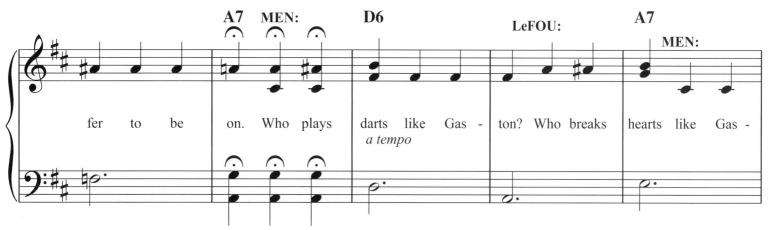

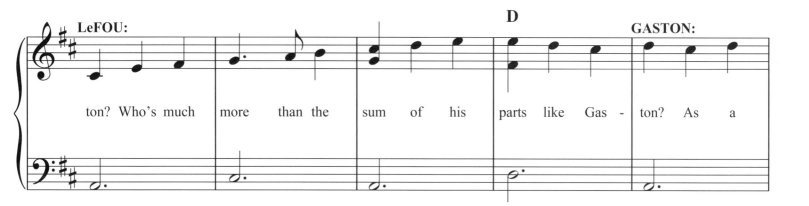

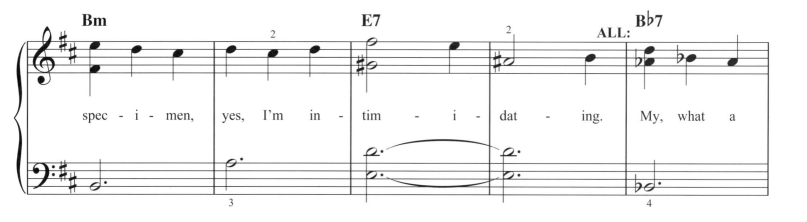

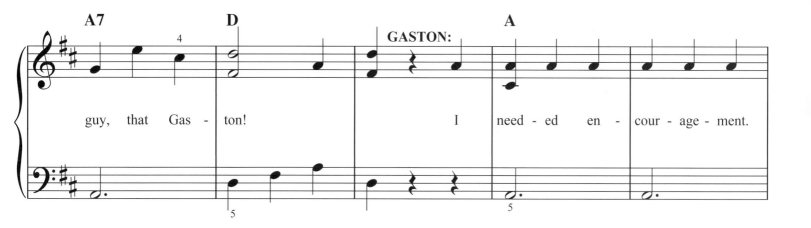

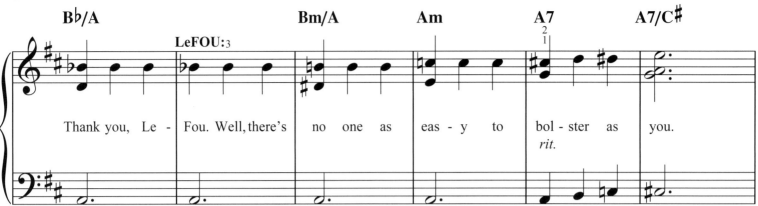

Thank you, Le - Fou. Well, there's no one as eas - y to bol - ster as you. *rit.*

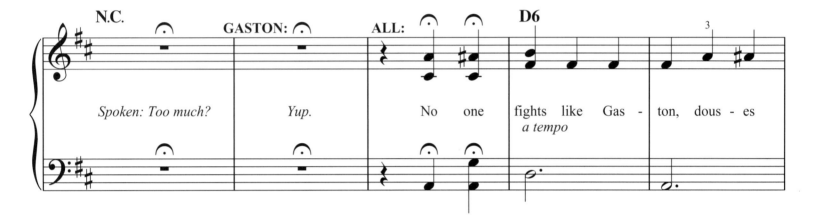

Spoken: Too much? *Yup.* No one fights like Gas - ton, dous - es *a tempo*

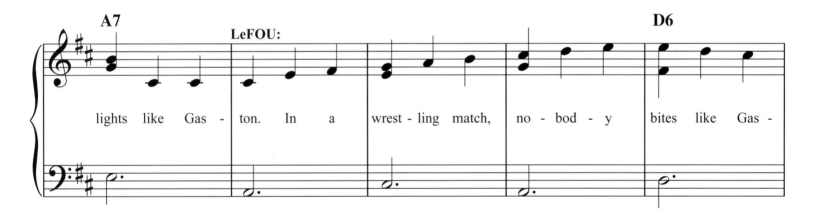

lights like Gas - ton. In a wrest - ling match, no - bod - y bites like Gas -

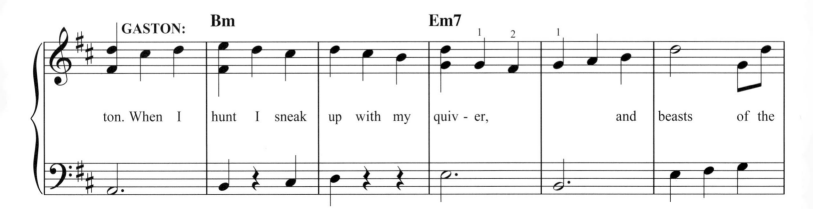

ton. When I hunt I sneak up with my quiv - er, and beasts of the

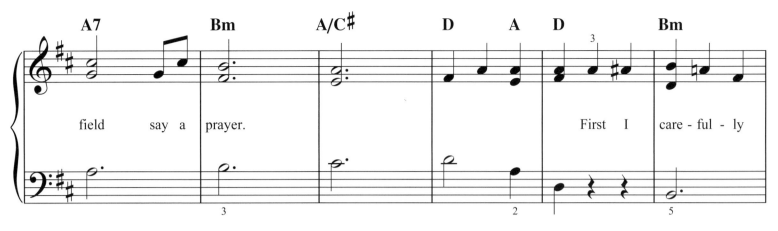

field say a prayer. First I care - ful - ly

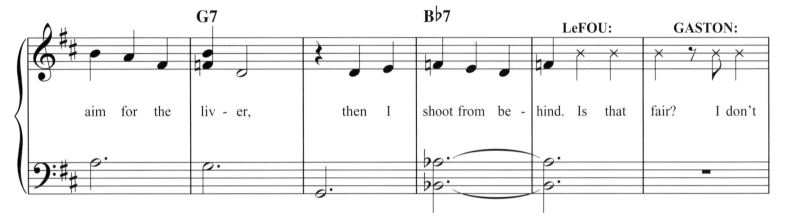

aim for the liv - er, then I shoot from be - hind. Is that fair? I don't

care. No one hits like Gas - ton, match - es wits like Gas -

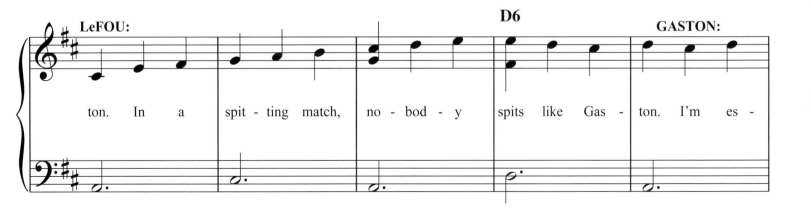

ton. In a spit - ting match, no - bod - y spits like Gas - ton. I'm es -

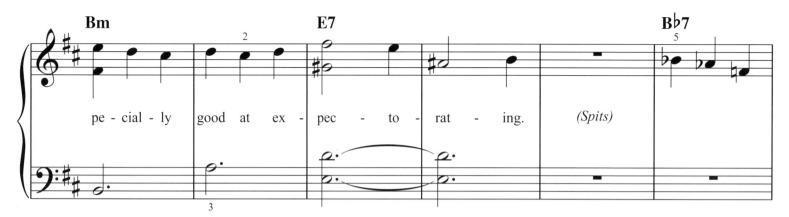

pe - cial - ly good at ex - pec - to - rat - ing. *(Spits)*

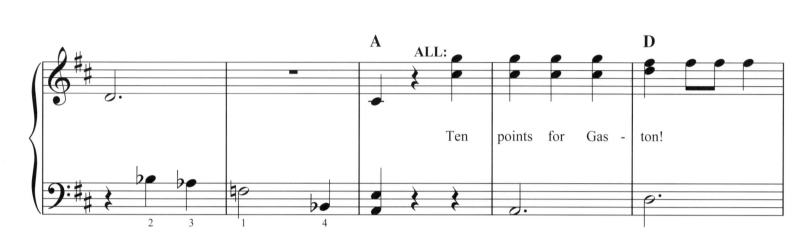

ALL:

Ten points for Gas - ton!

GASTON:

When I was a lad I ate

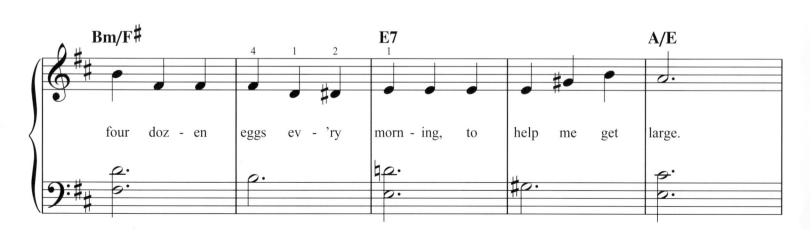

four doz - en eggs ev - 'ry morn - ing, to help me get large.

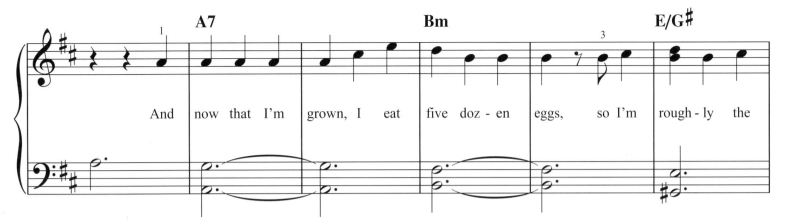

And now that I'm grown, I eat five doz-en eggs, so I'm rough-ly the

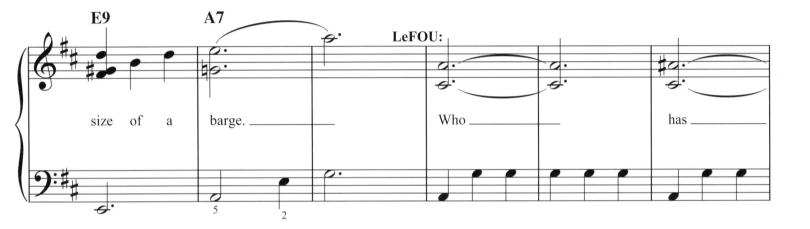

size of a barge. _____ Who _____ has _____

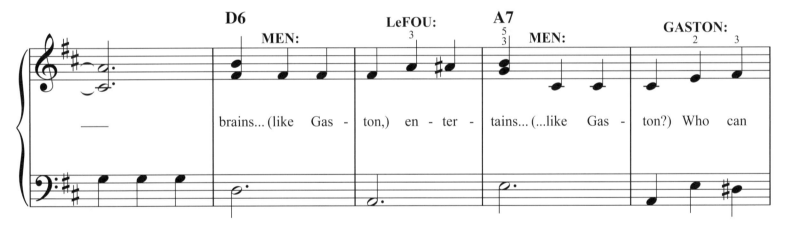

_____ brains... (like Gas-ton,) en-ter-tains... (...like Gas-ton?) Who can

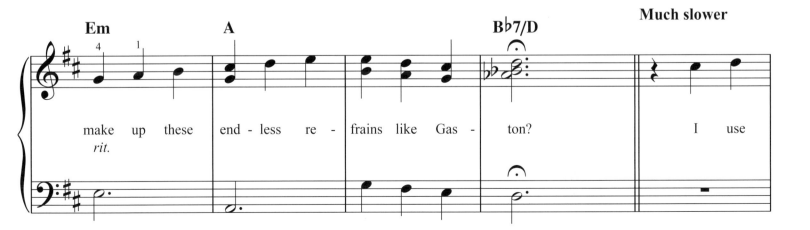

make up these end-less re-frains like Gas-ton? I use

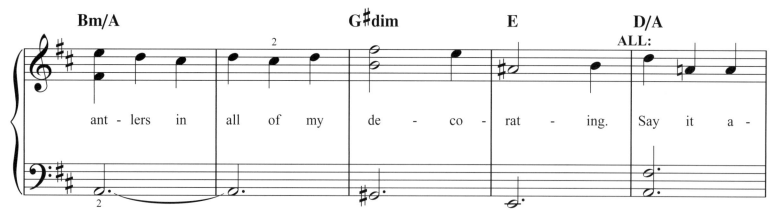

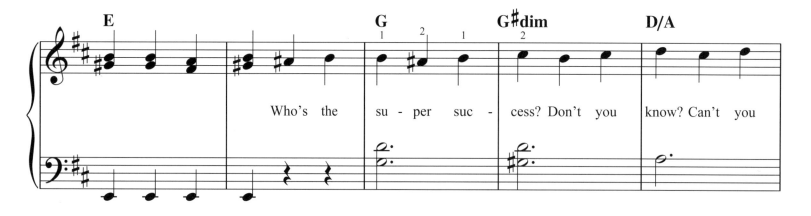

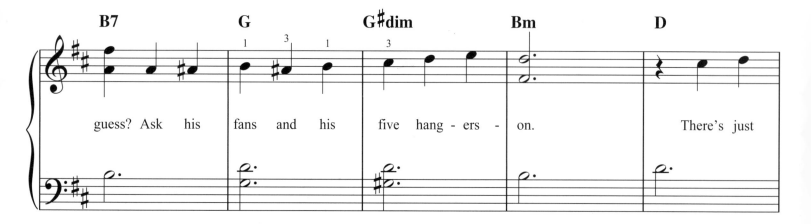

one guy in town who's got all of it down. And his

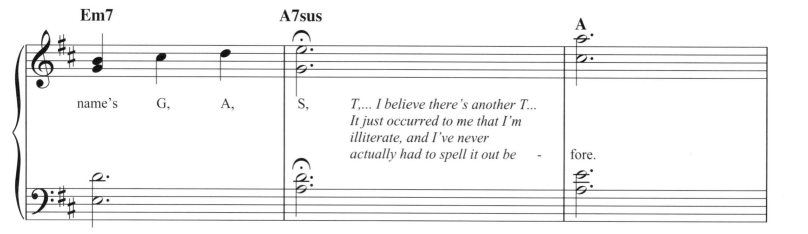

name's G, A, S, *T,... I believe there's another T...*
It just occurred to me that I'm
illiterate, and I've never
actually had to spell it out be - fore.

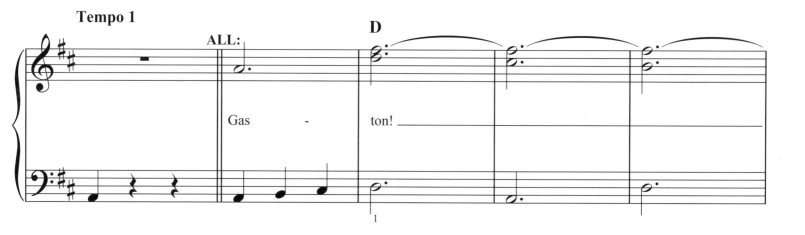

Tempo 1

ALL:

Gas - ton! _____

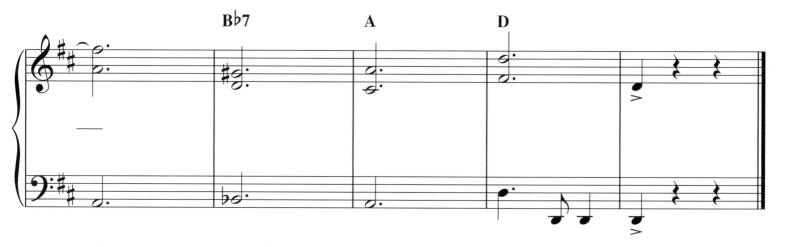

BE OUR GUEST

Music by ALAN MENKEN
Lyrics by HOWARD ASHMAN

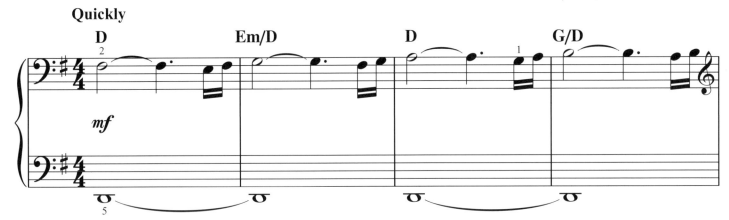

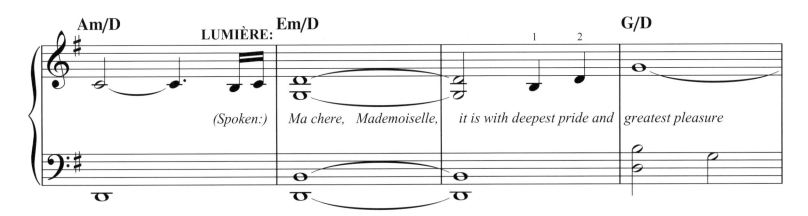

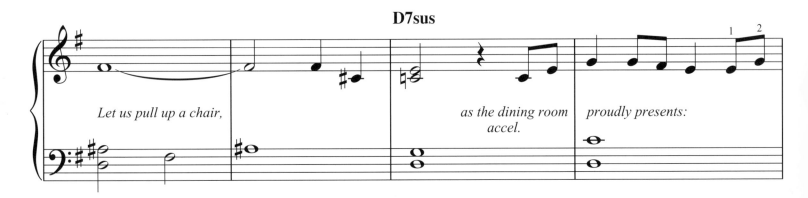

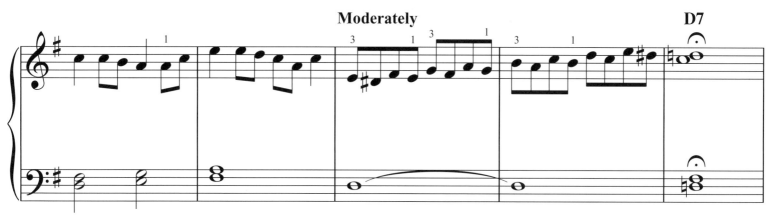

Moderately   D7

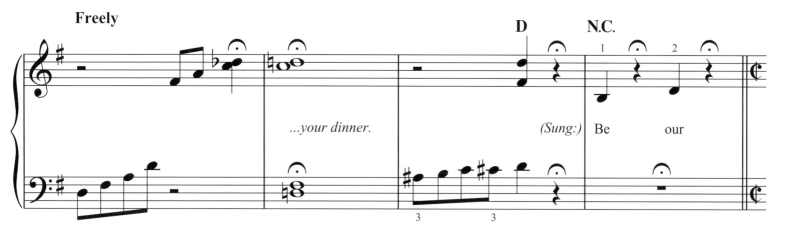

Freely   D   N.C.

...your dinner.

(Sung:) Be our

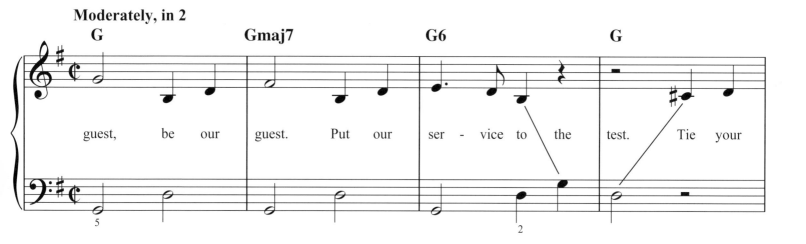

Moderately, in 2

G   Gmaj7   G6   G

guest,   be our guest. Put our ser - vice to the test. Tie your

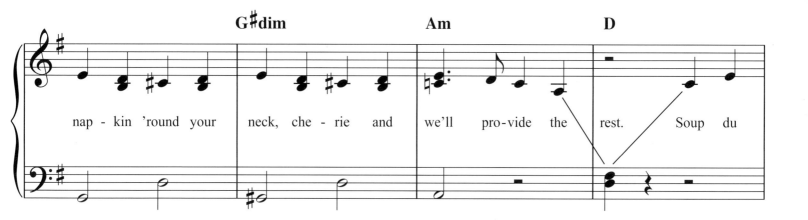

G#dim   Am   D

nap - kin 'round your neck, che - rie and we'll pro-vide the rest. Soup du

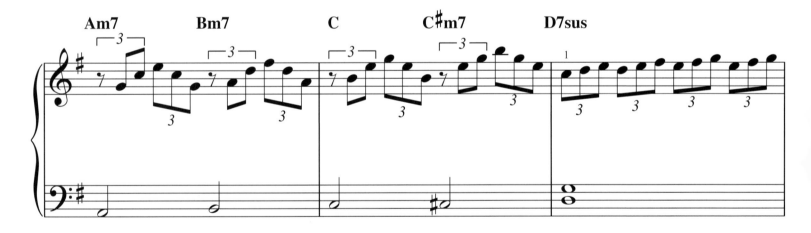

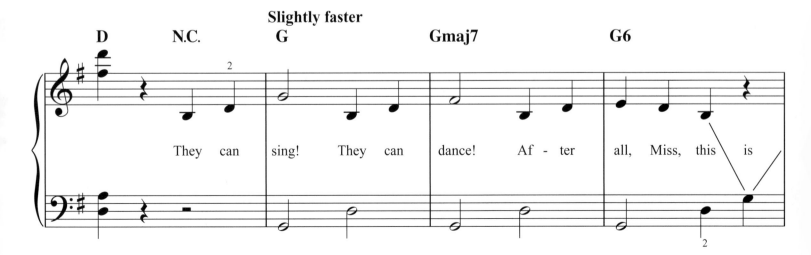

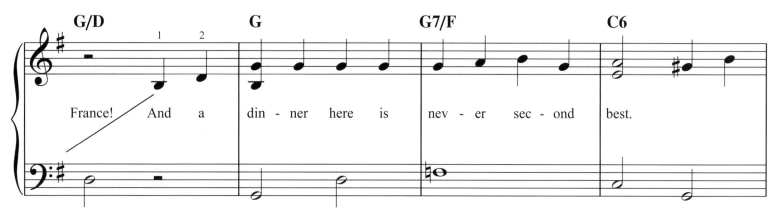

France! And a din - ner here is nev - er sec - ond best.

Go on, un - fold your men - u, take a glance, and then ___

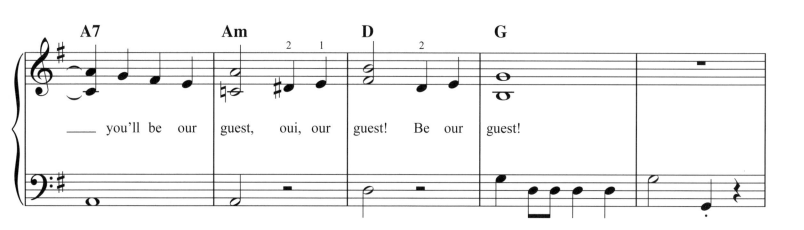

___ you'll be our guest, oui, our guest! Be our guest!

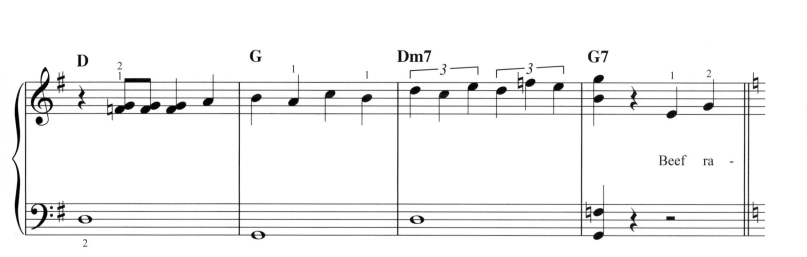

Beef ra -

Slightly faster

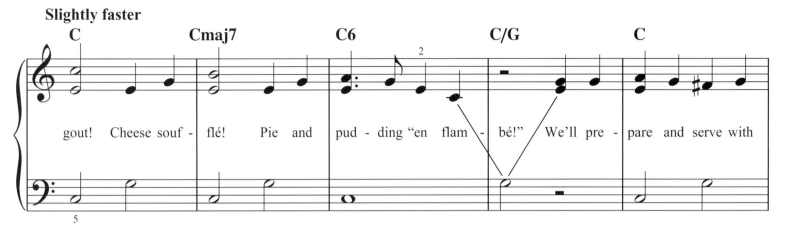

gout! Cheese souf - flé! Pie and pud - ding "en flam - bé!" We'll pre - pare and serve with

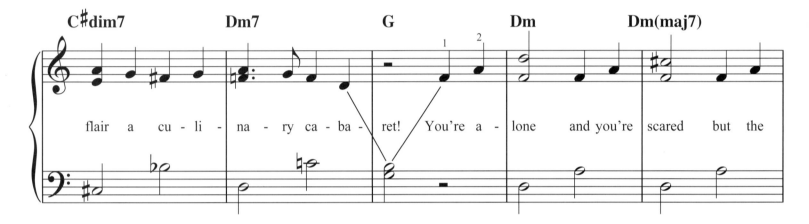

flair a cu - li - na - ry ca - ba - ret! You're a - lone and you're scared but the

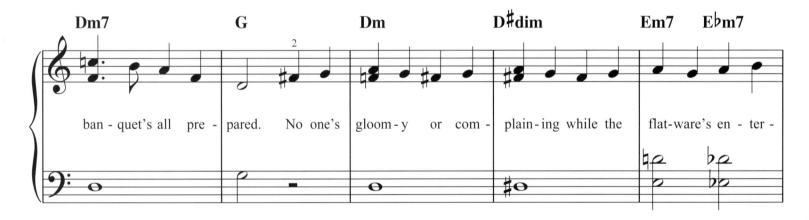

ban - quet's all pre - pared. No one's gloom - y or com - plain - ing while the flat-ware's en - ter -

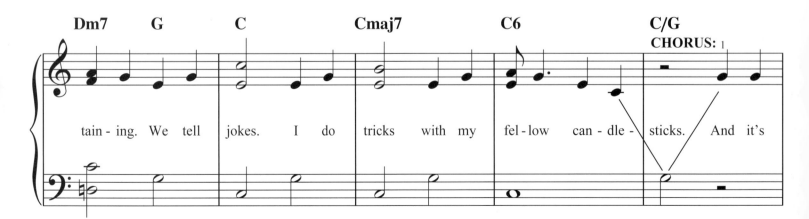

tain - ing. We tell jokes. I do tricks with my fel - low can - dle - sticks. And it's

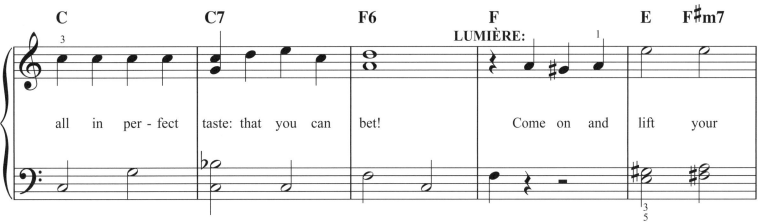

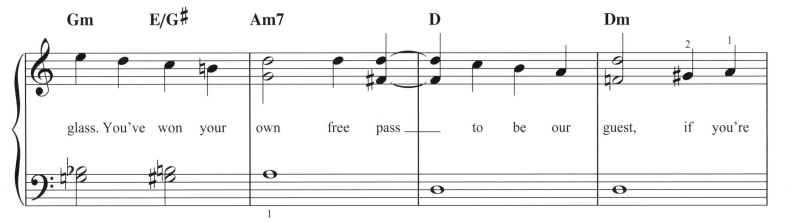

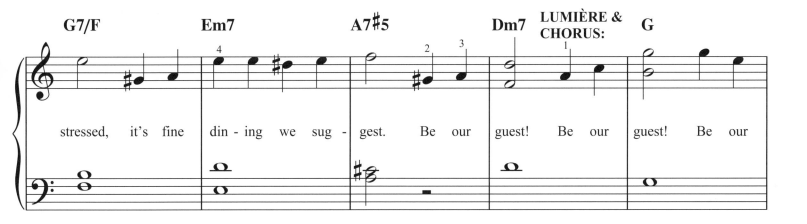

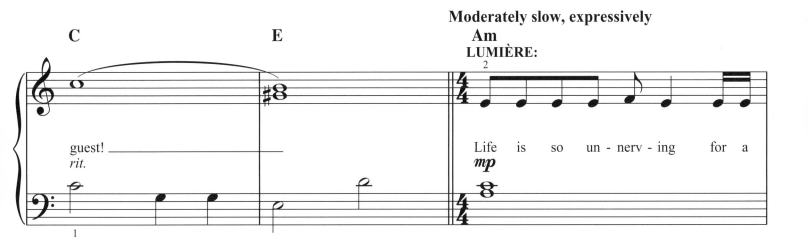

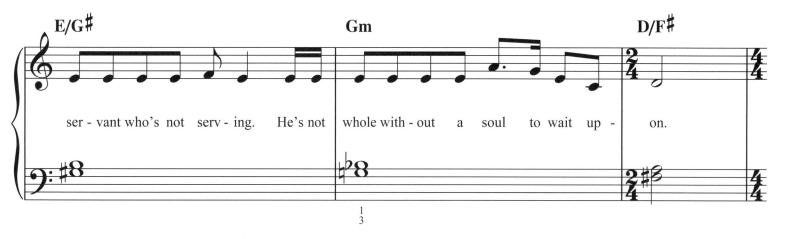

ser - vant who's not serv - ing. He's not whole with - out a soul to wait up - on.

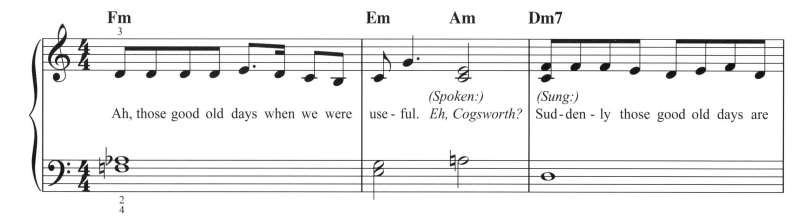

Ah, those good old days when we were use - ful. *Eh, Cogsworth?* *(Sung:)* Sud - den - ly those good old days are

(Spoken:)

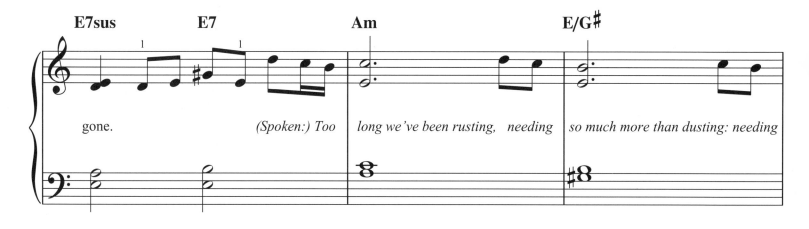

gone. *(Spoken:)* Too long we've been rusting, needing so much more than dusting: needing

exercise, a chance to use our *skills!*

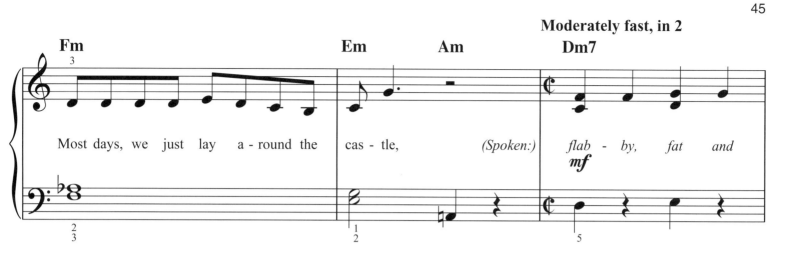

Most days, we just lay a-round the cas-tle, *(Spoken:)* *flab - by,* *fat* *and*

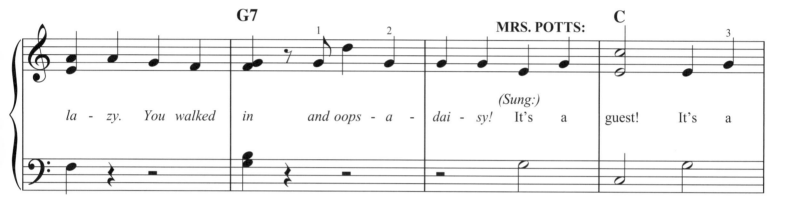

la - zy. *You walked* *in* *and oops - a - dai - sy!* It's a guest! It's a

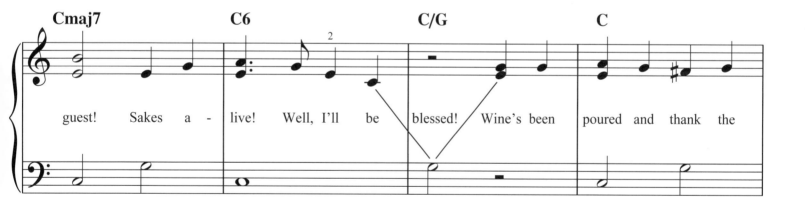

guest! Sakes a - live! Well, I'll be blessed! Wine's been poured and thank the

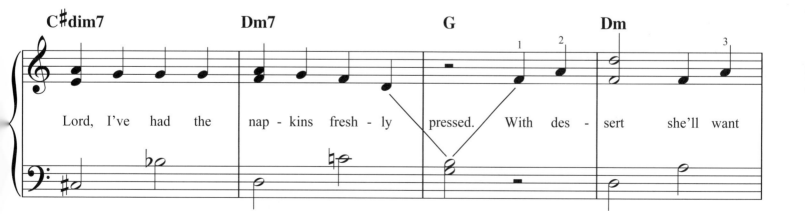

Lord, I've had the nap - kins fresh - ly pressed. With des - sert she'll want

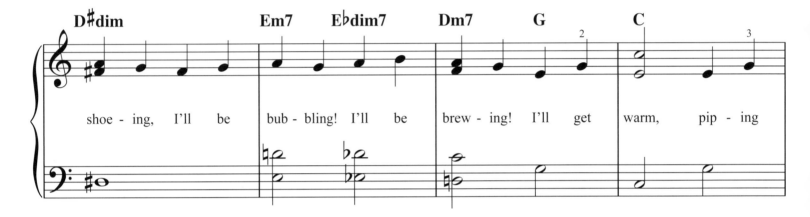

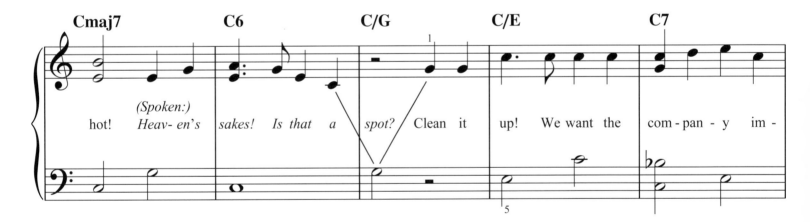

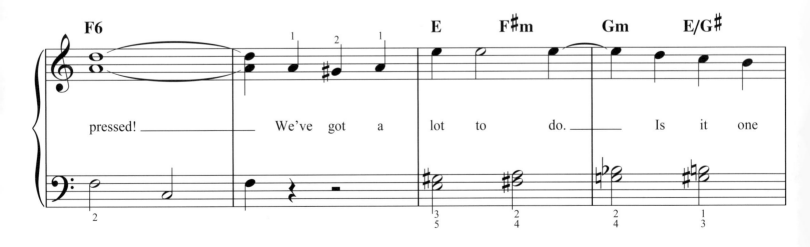

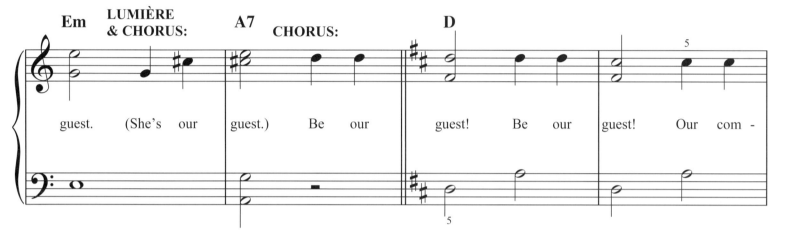

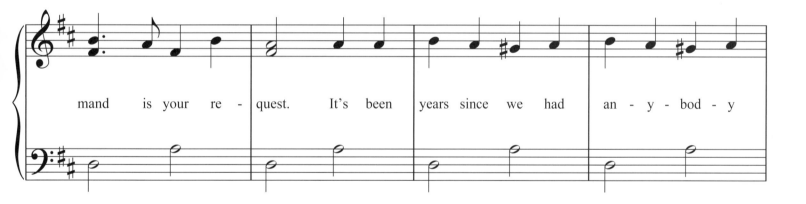

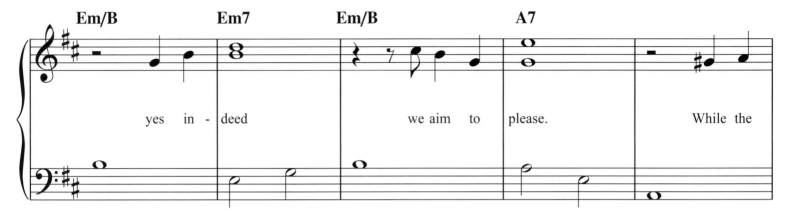

yes in - deed   we aim to please.   While the

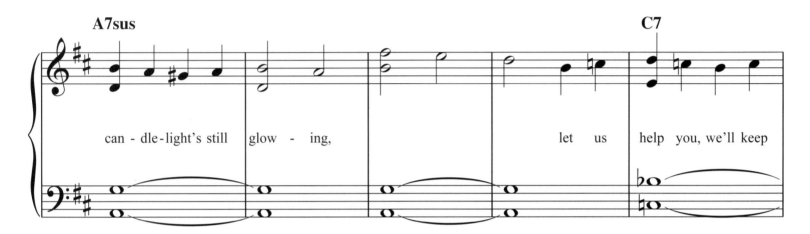

can - dle - light's still   glow - ing,   let us help you, we'll keep

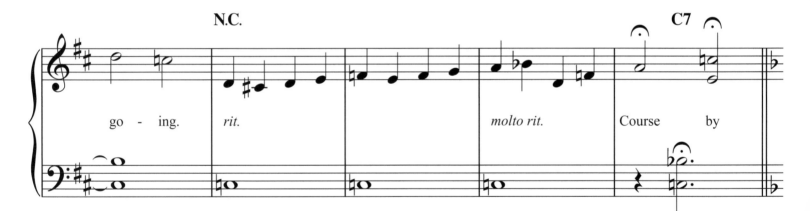

go - ing.   *rit.*   *molto rit.*   Course   by

Slowly

course,   one   by   one,   'til you   shout,   "E - nough! I'm   done!"   Then we'll

accel.

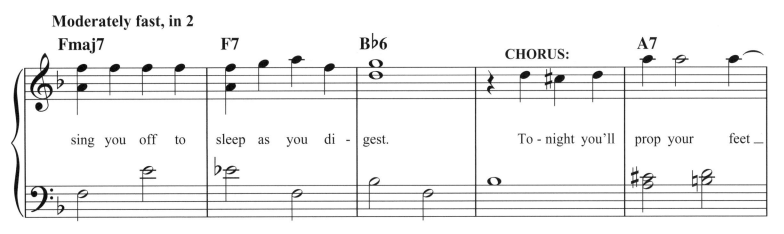

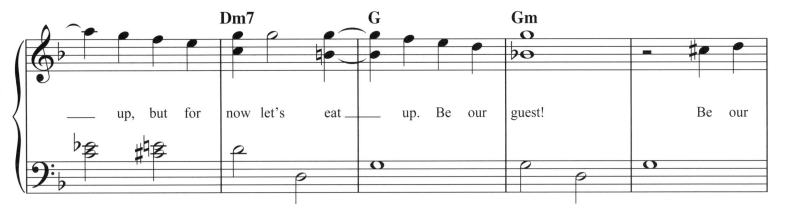

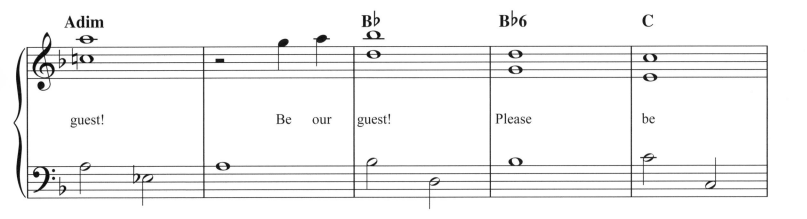

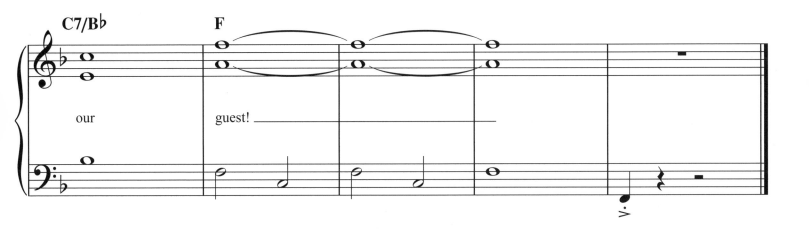

DAYS IN THE SUN

Music by ALAN MENKEN
Lyrics by TIM RICE

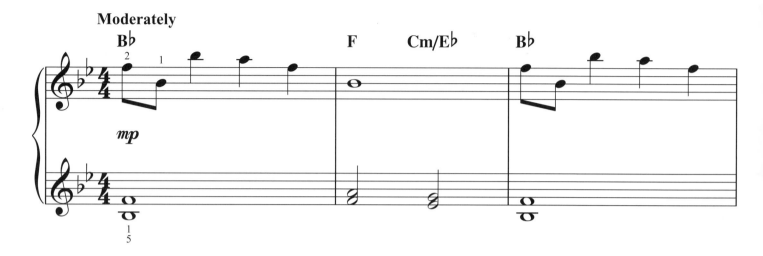

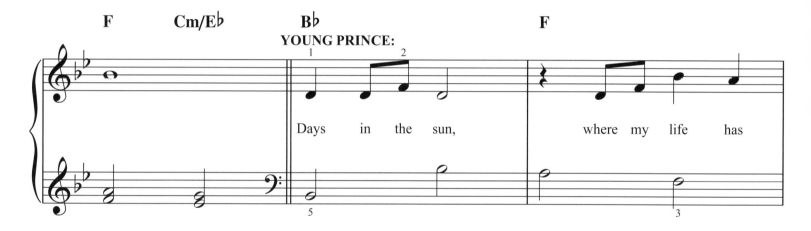

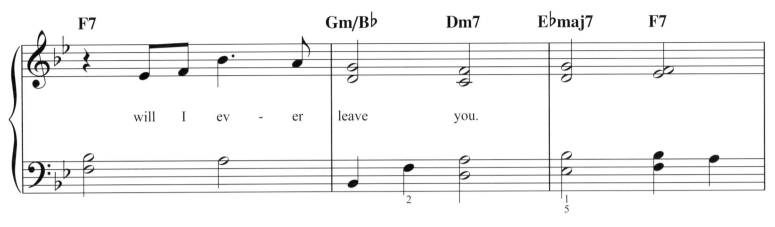

will I ev - er leave you.

Will I trem - ble a - gain

to my dear one's gor - geous re - frain? Will you now for -

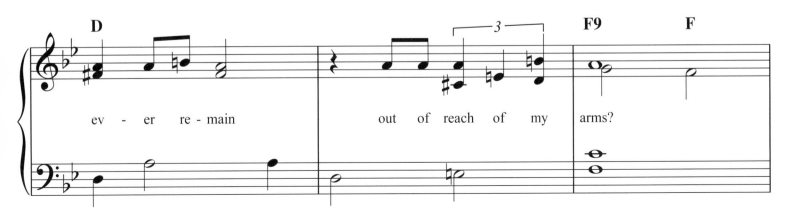

ev - er re - main out of reach of my arms?

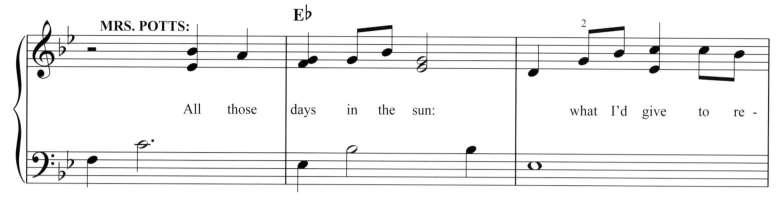

MRS. POTTS:
All those days in the sun: what I'd give to re-

live just one, _____ un - do what's done

and bring back the light. **MADAME GARDEROBE:** Oh,

I could sing of the pain these dark days

Dm / **E♭maj7** / **B♭/D**

bring, the spell we're un - der.

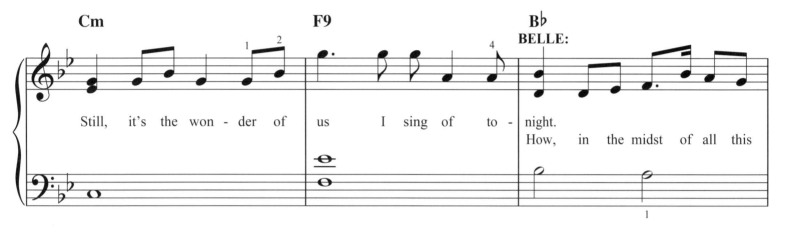

Cm / **F9** / **B♭** **BELLE:**

Still, it's the won - der of us I sing of to - night. How, in the midst of all this

Gm **F** / **E♭** / **B♭/D** **Dm7/G**

sor - row, can so much hope and love en - dure? I was

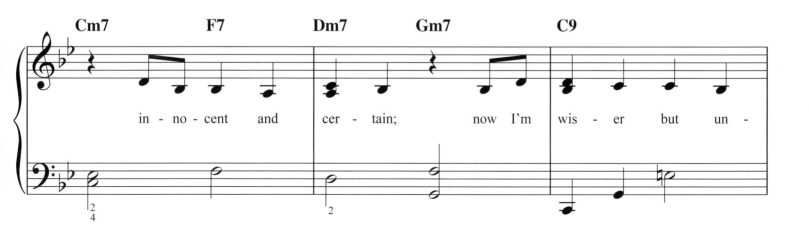

Cm7 **F7** **Dm7** **Gm7** **C9**

in - no - cent and cer - tain; now I'm wis - er but un -

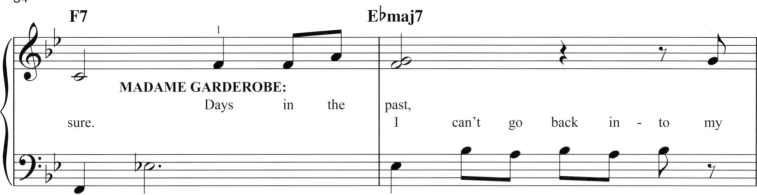

MADAME GARDEROBE:

Days in the past,
sure.

I can't go back in-to my

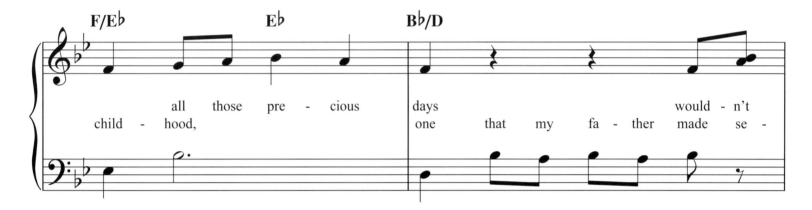

all those pre - cious days
child - hood,
one that my fa - ther made se -

would - n't

last.
cure.

I can feel a change in me. I'm

strong - er now, but still not free.
rall.

Days in the sun
$\boldsymbol{f}$ *a tempo*

5

will re - turn, we must be - lieve, as

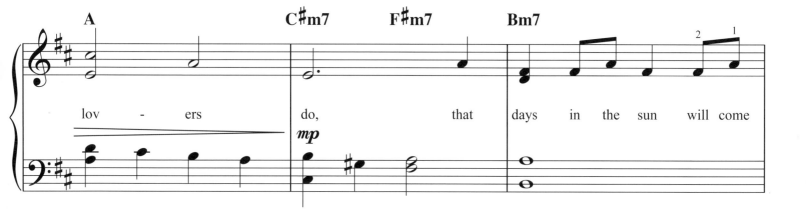

lov - ers do, that days in the sun will come

_mp_

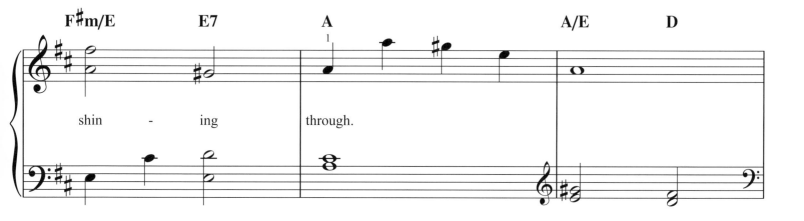

shin - ing through.

molto rit.

SOMETHING THERE

Music by ALAN MENKEN
Lyrics by HOWARD ASHMAN

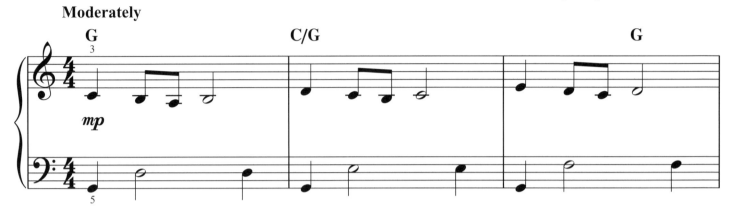

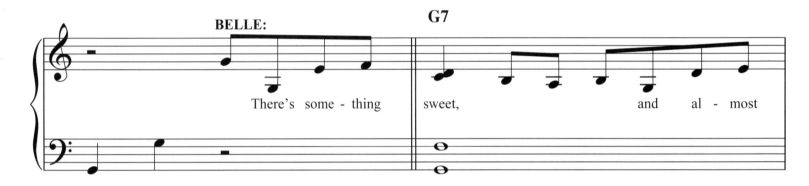

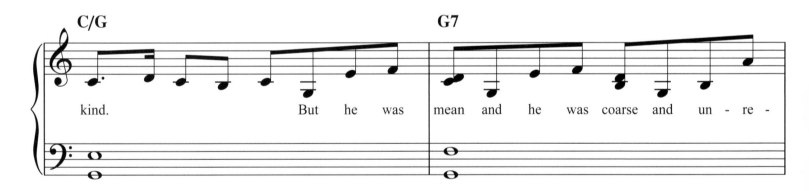

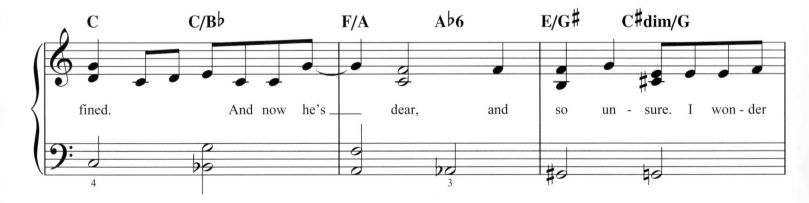

why I did - n't see it there be - fore.

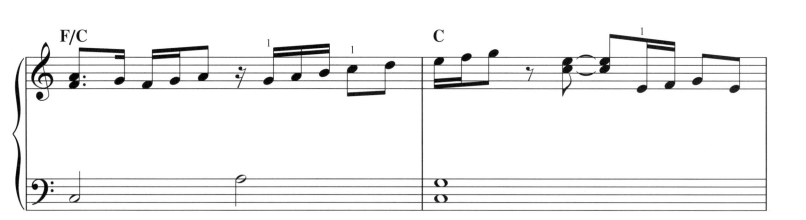

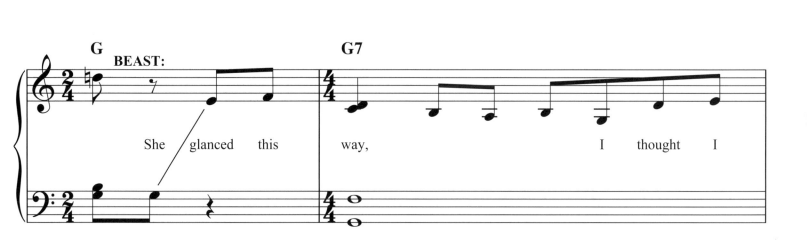

She glanced this way, I thought I

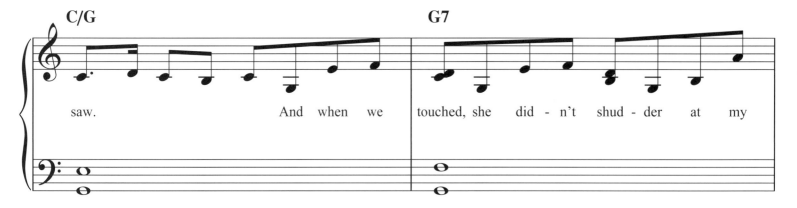

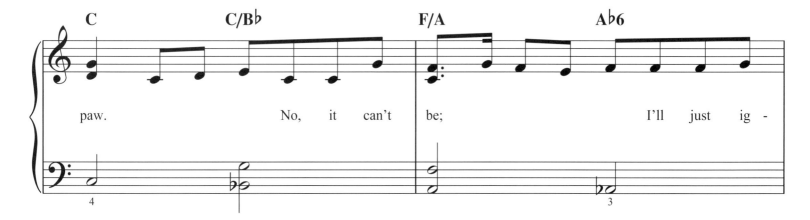

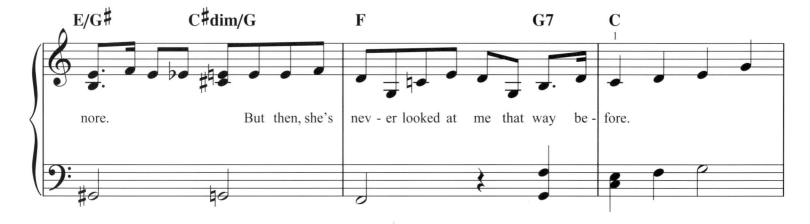

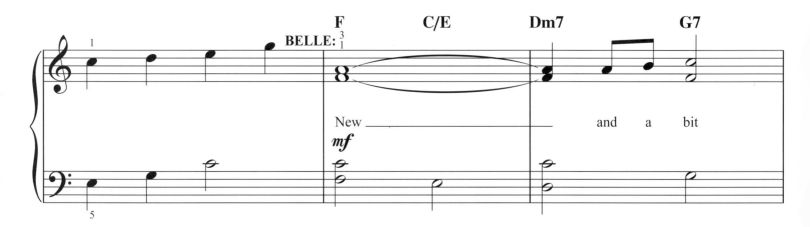

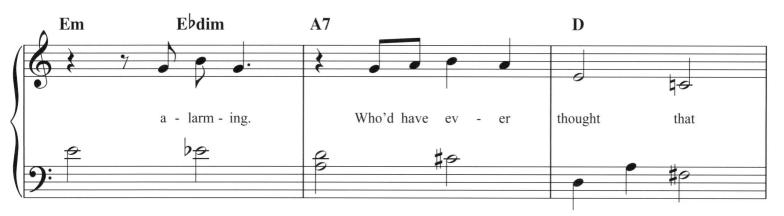

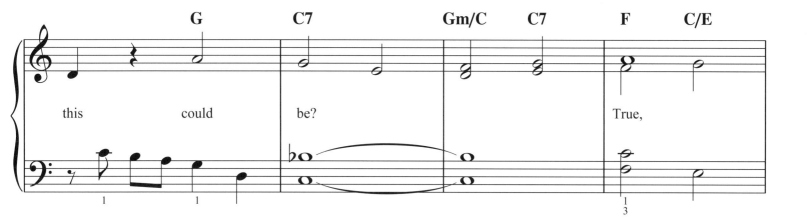

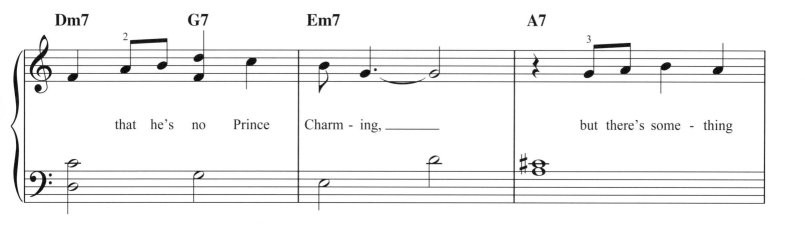

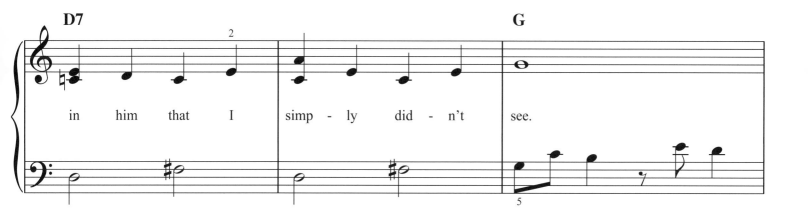

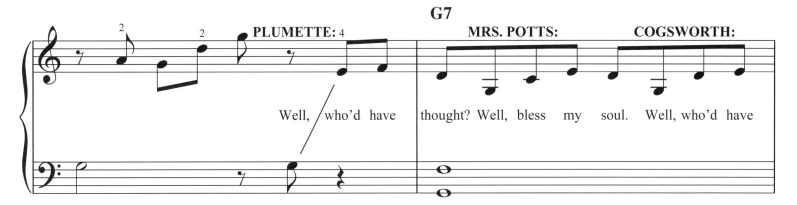

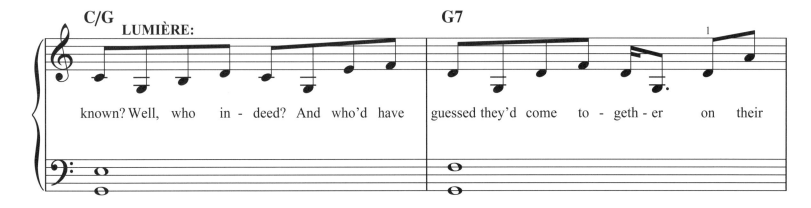

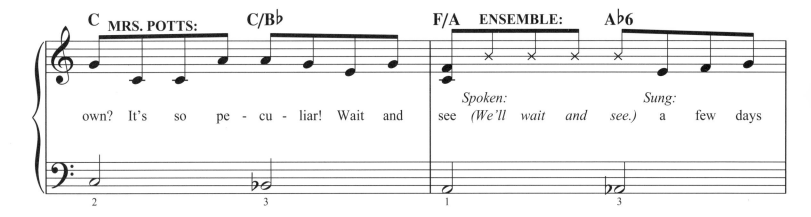

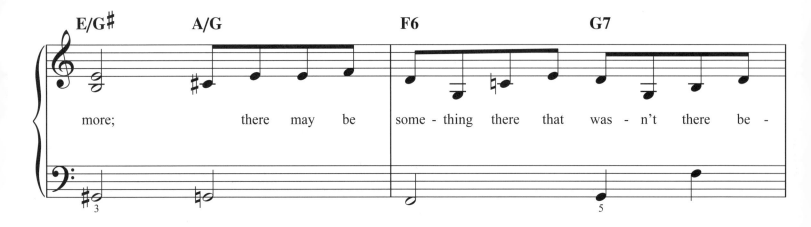

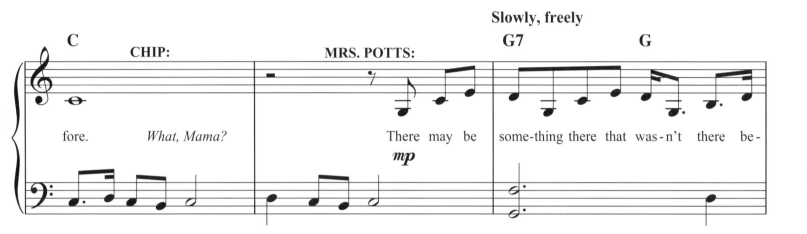

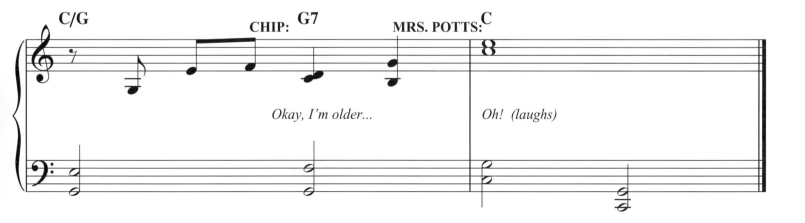

THE MOB SONG

Music by ALAN MENKEN
Lyrics by HOWARD ASHMAN

Moderately fast

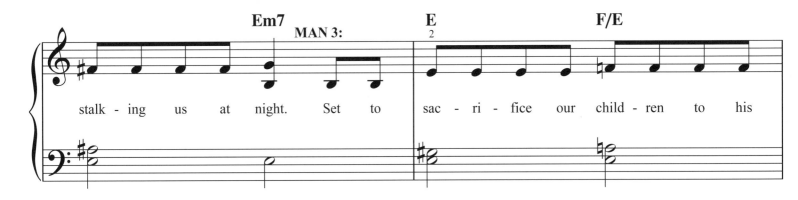

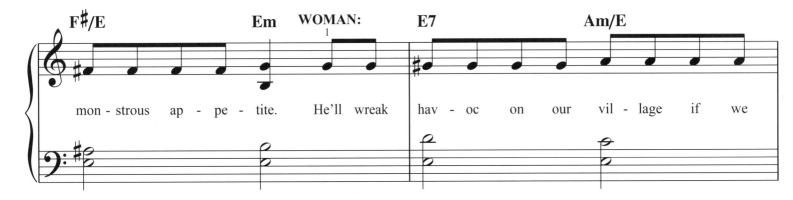

let him wan-der free. So it's time to take some ac-tion boys, it's

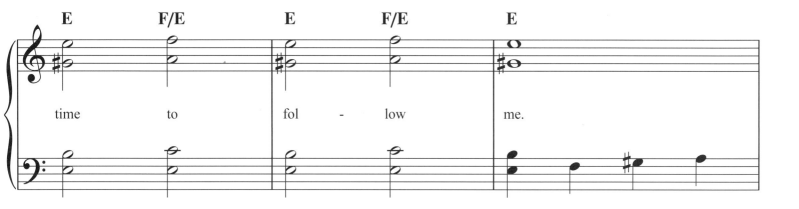

time to fol - low me.

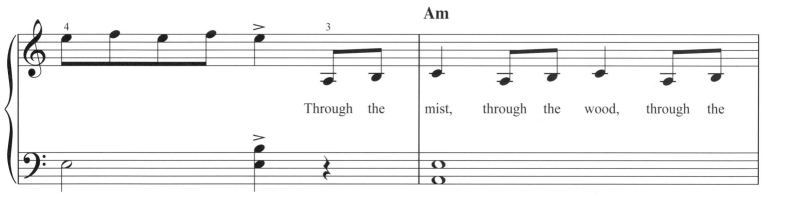

Through the mist, through the wood, through the

dark-ness and the shad-ows, it's a night-mare, but it's one ex-cit-ing

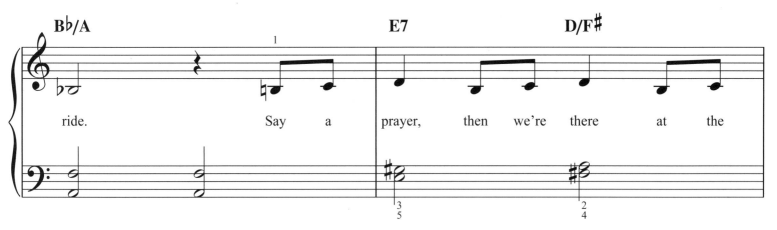

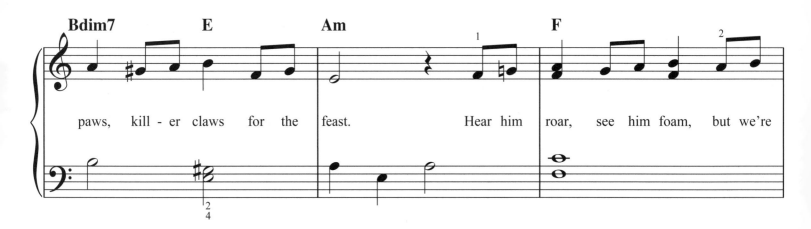

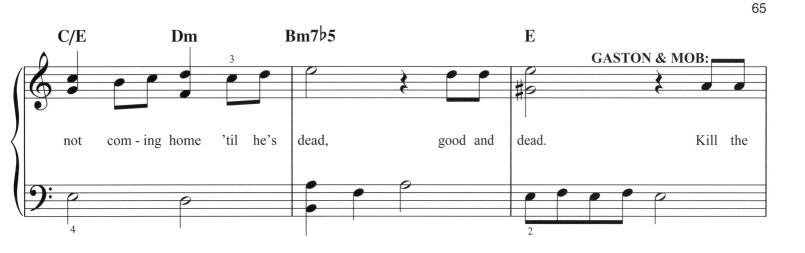

not com-ing home 'til he's dead, good and dead. Kill the

beast! Light your torch! Mount your horse: Screw your

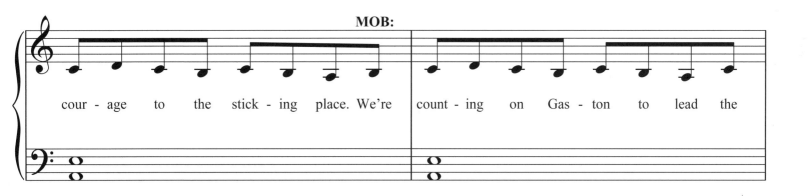

cour-age to the stick-ing place. We're count-ing on Gas-ton to lead the

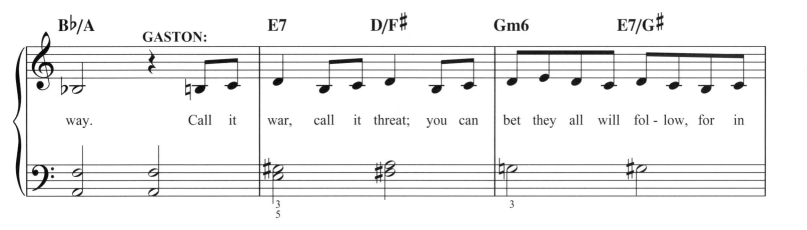

way. Call it war, call it threat; you can bet they all will fol-low, for in

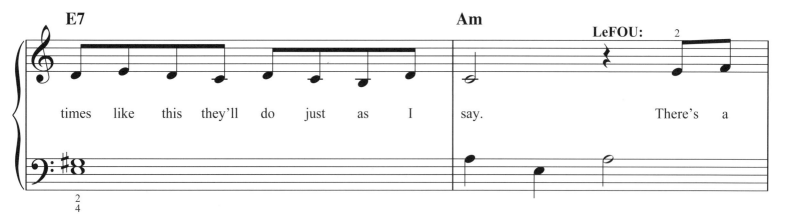

times like this they'll do just as I say. There's a

beast run - ning wild, there's no ques - tion. But I fear the wrong mon - ster's re -

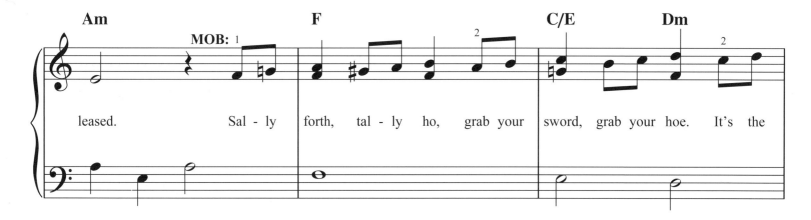

leased. Sal - ly forth, tal - ly ho, grab your sword, grab your hoe. It's the

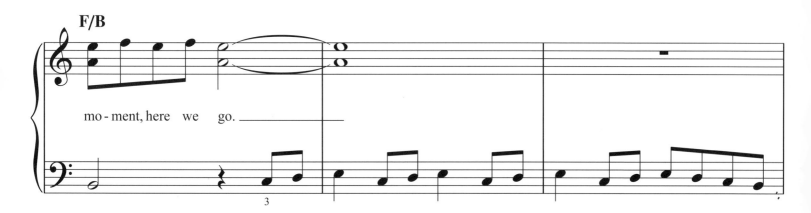

mo - ment, here we go. _____

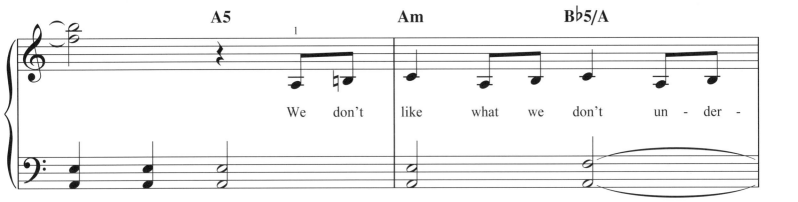

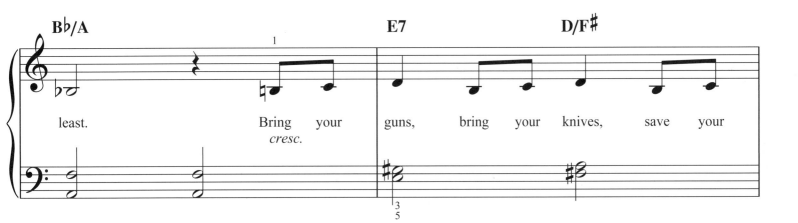

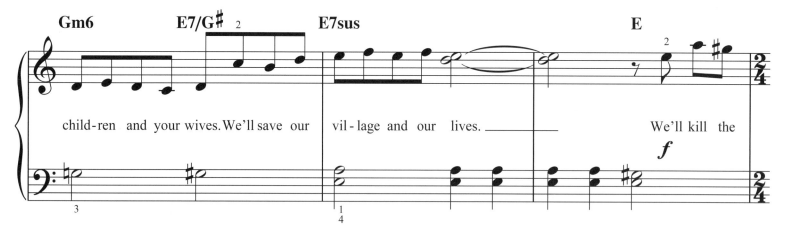

child-ren and your wives. We'll save our vil-lage and our lives. _____ We'll kill the

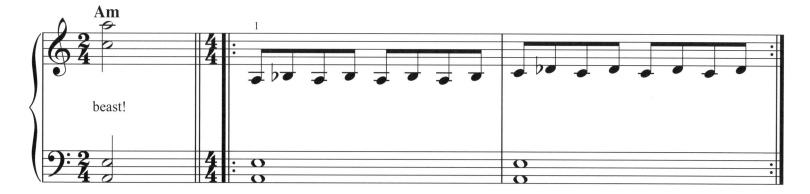

beast!

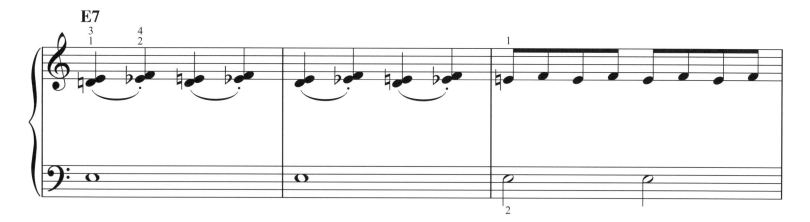

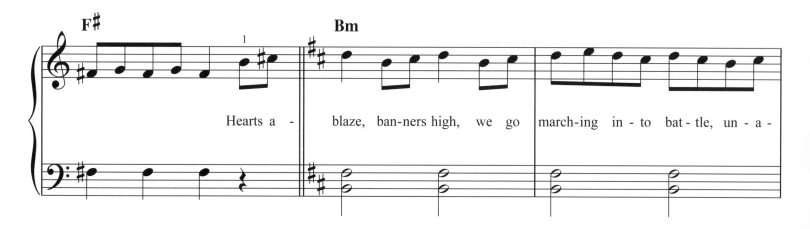

Hearts a - blaze, ban-ners high, we go march-ing in-to bat - tle, un-a-

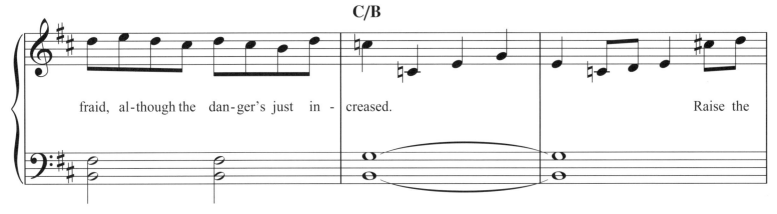

fraid, al-though the dan-ger's just in - creased. Raise the

C/B

flag, sing the song. Here we come: we're fif - ty strong, and fif - ty

F#7   **E/G#**   **Am6**   **F#7/A#**

French - men can't be wrong! _____ *(Shouted:) Let's kill the*

F#7sus

beast!   *Kill the beast!*   *Kill the beast!*

B

HOW DOES A MOMENT LAST FOREVER

(As performed by Celine Dion)

Music by ALAN MENKEN
Lyrics by TIM RICE

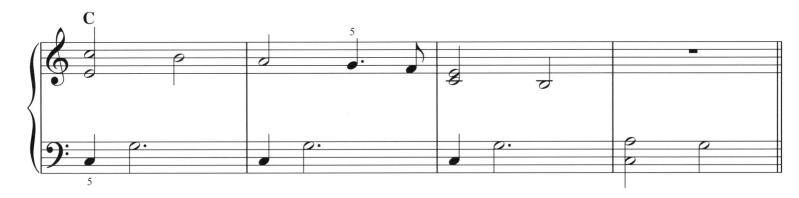

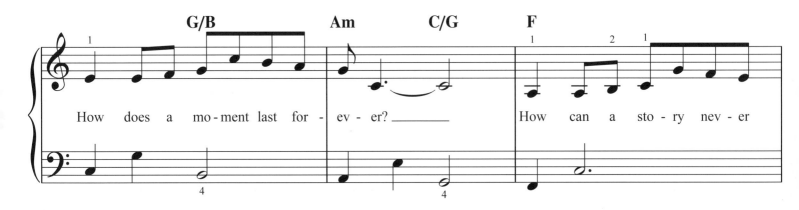

How does a mo-ment last for-ev-er? _____ How can a sto-ry nev-er

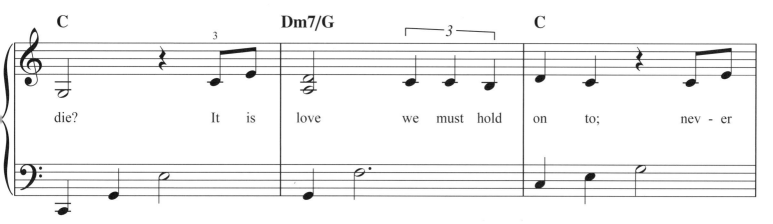

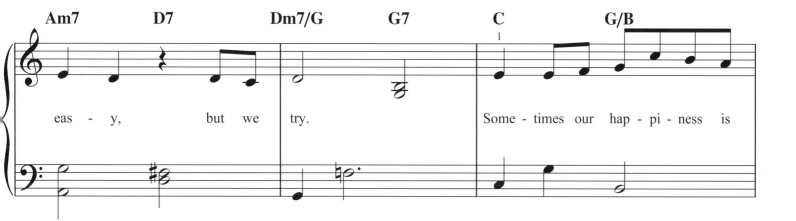

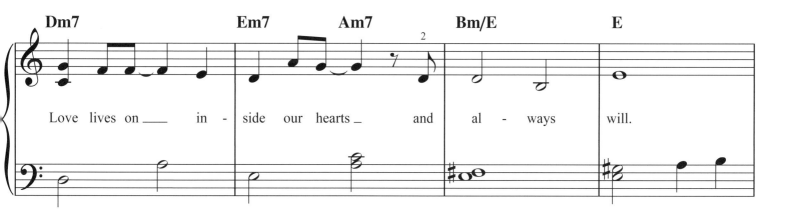

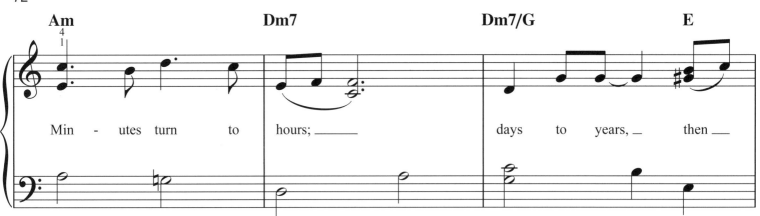

Min - utes turn to hours; _____ days to years, _ then ___ gone.

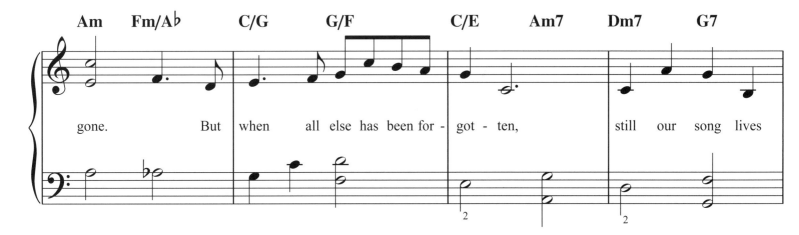

But when all else has been for - got - ten, still our song lives on.

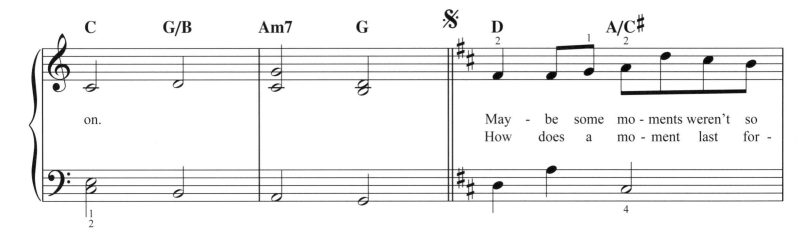

May - be some mo - ments weren't so
How does a mo - ment last for -

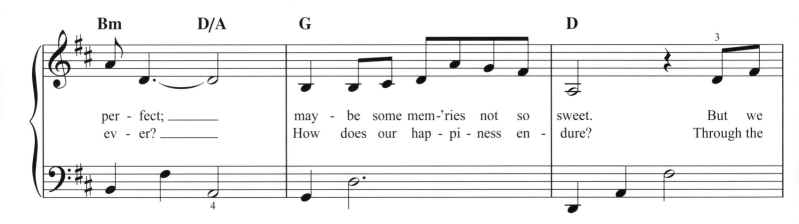

per - fect; _____ may - be some mem - 'ries not so sweet. But we
ev - er? _____ How does our hap - pi - ness en - dure? Through the

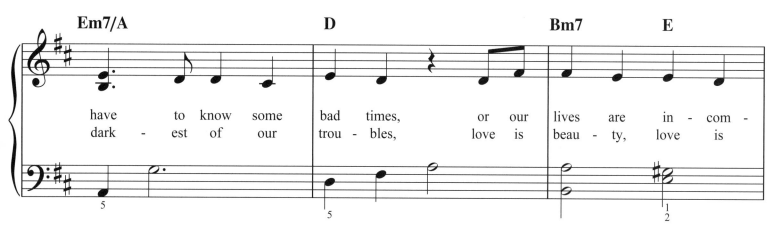

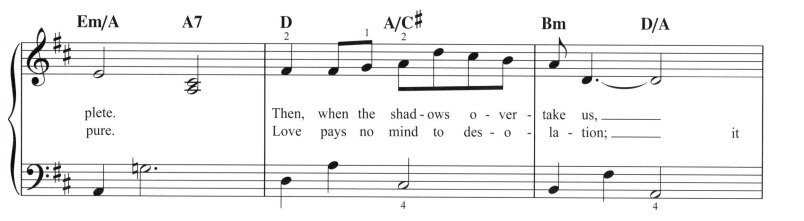

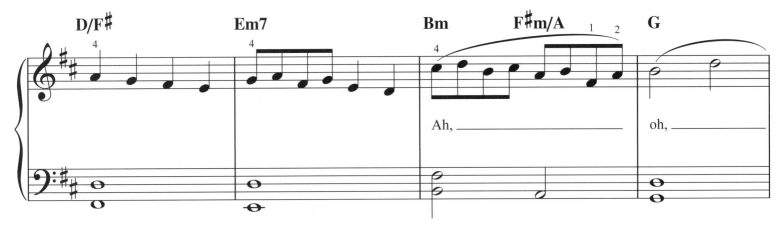

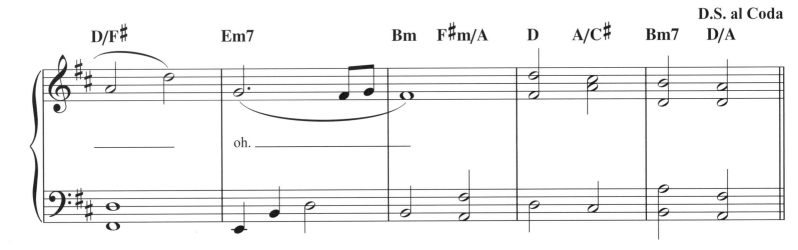

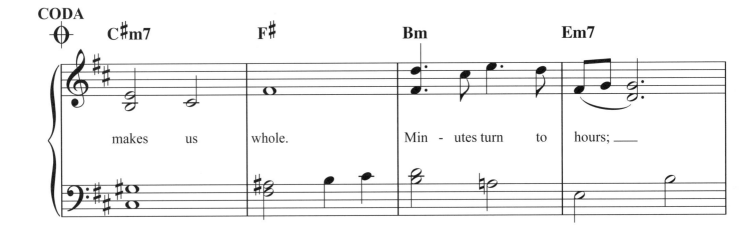

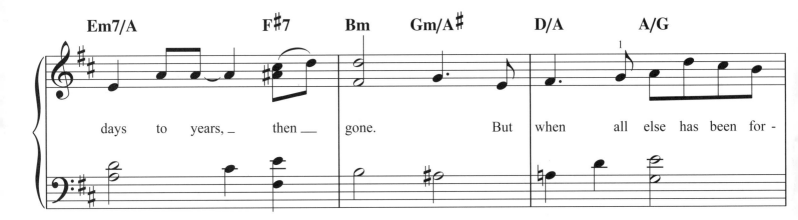

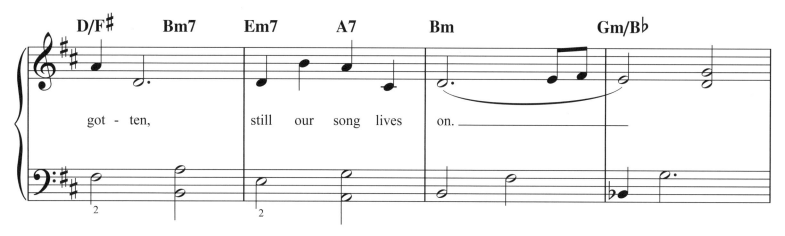

got - ten, still our song lives on. ____

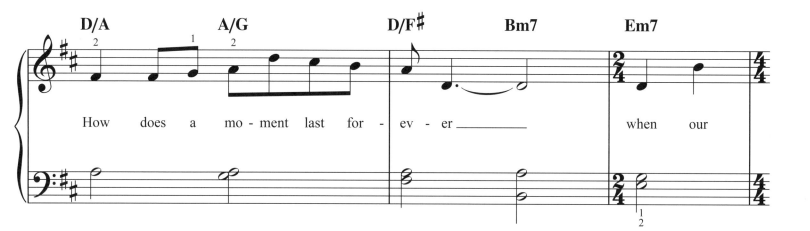

How does a mo - ment last for - ev - er ____ when our

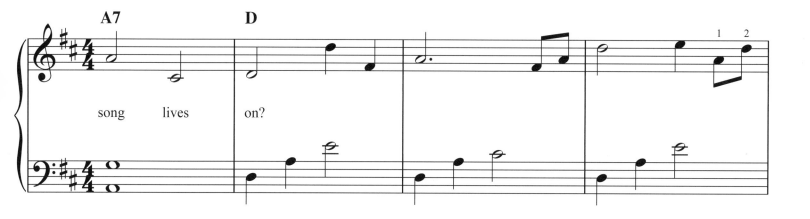

song lives on?

BEAUTY AND THE BEAST
(As performed by Ariana Grande and John Legend)

Music by ALAN MENKEN
Lyrics by HOWARD ASHMAN

Moderately slow

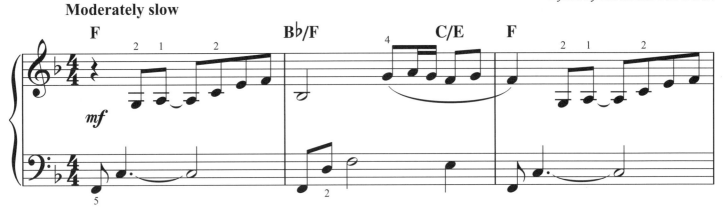

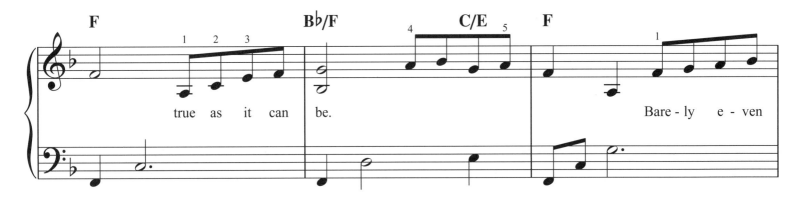

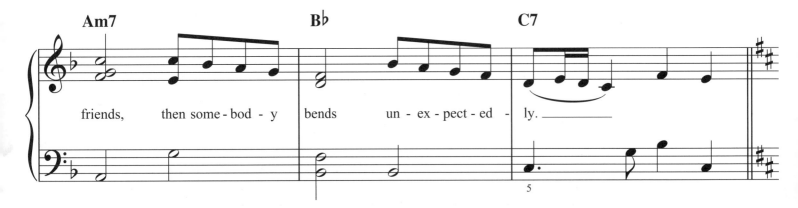

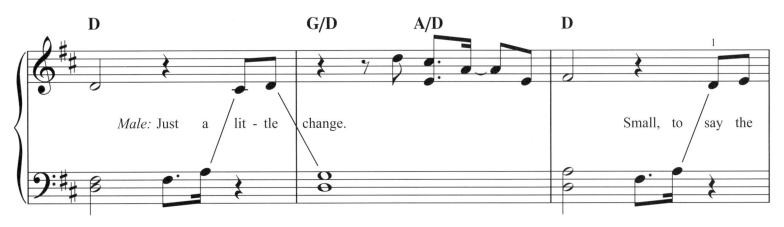

D **G/D** **A/D** **D**

Male: Just a lit - tle change.

Small, to say the

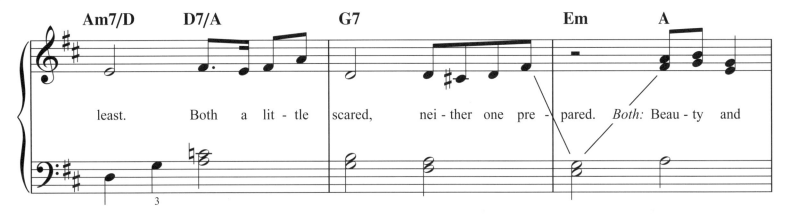

Am7/D **D7/A** **G7** **Em** **A**

least. Both a lit - tle scared, nei - ther one pre - pared. *Both:* Beau - ty and

D **F#m7**

the ___ Beast.

Ev - er just the same.

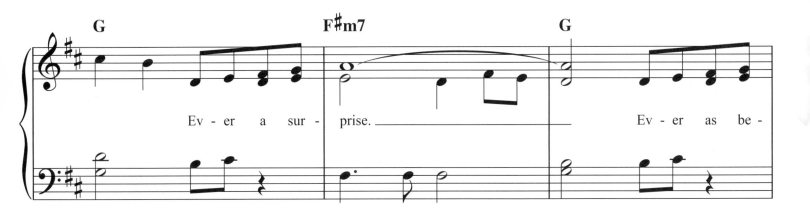

G **F#m7** **G**

Ev - er a sur - prise. ___

Ev - er as be -

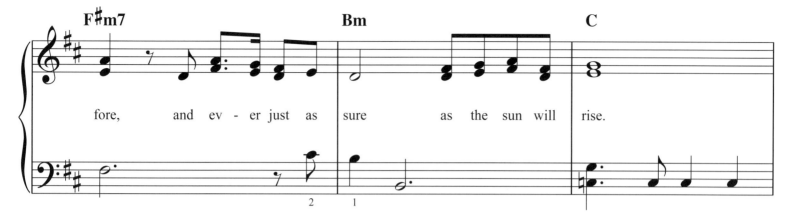

fore, and ev - er just as sure as the sun will rise.

Lead vocals ad lib.

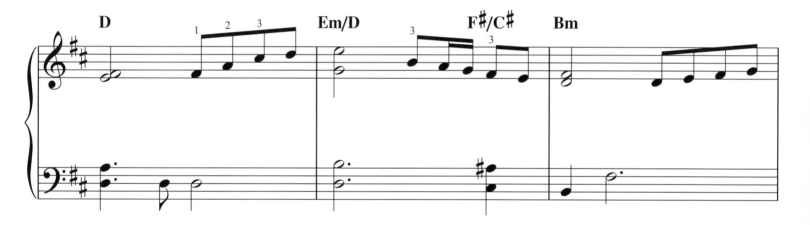

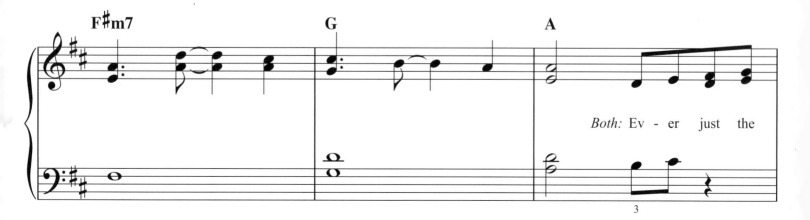

Both: Ev - er just the

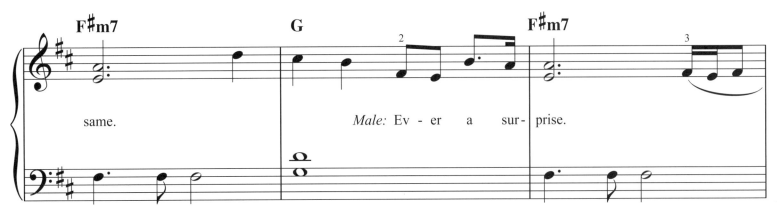

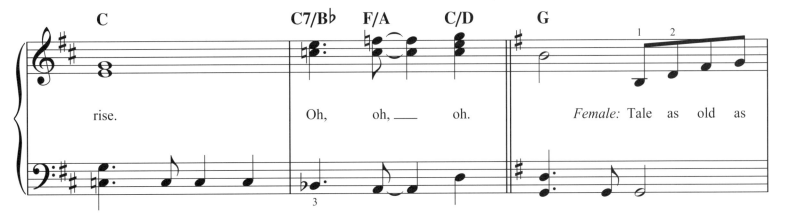

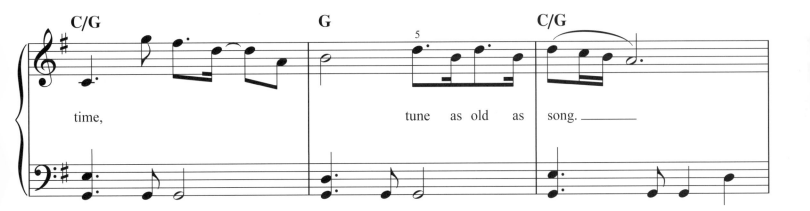

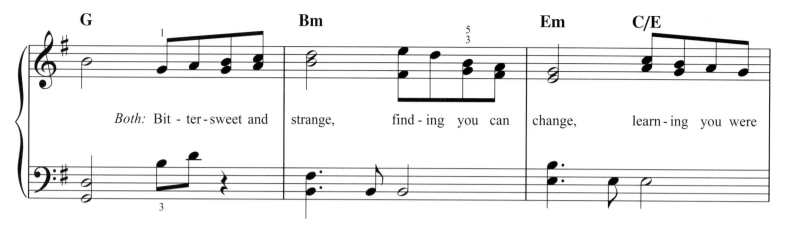

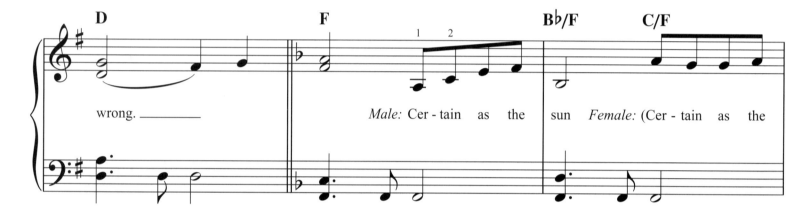

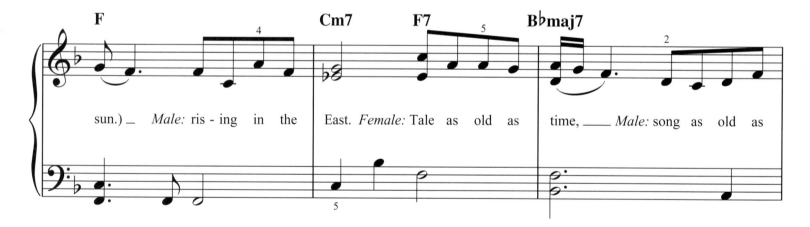

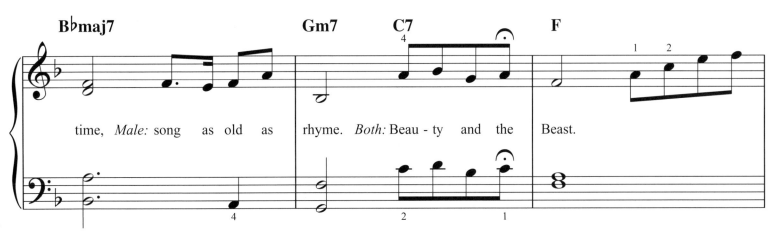

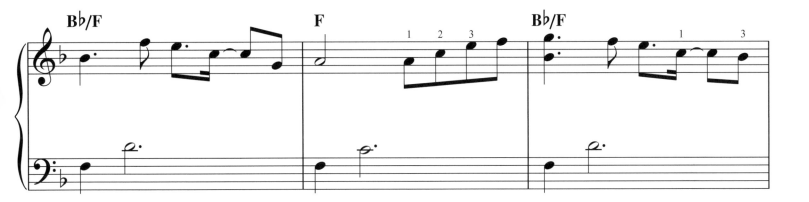

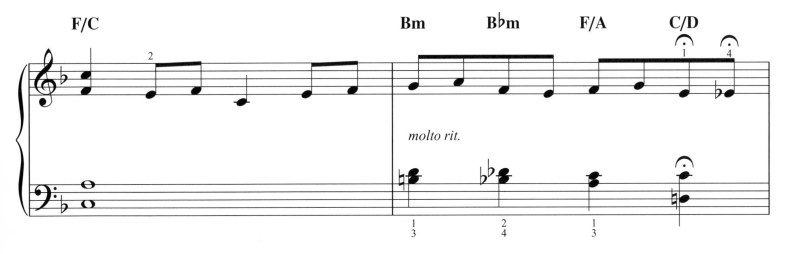

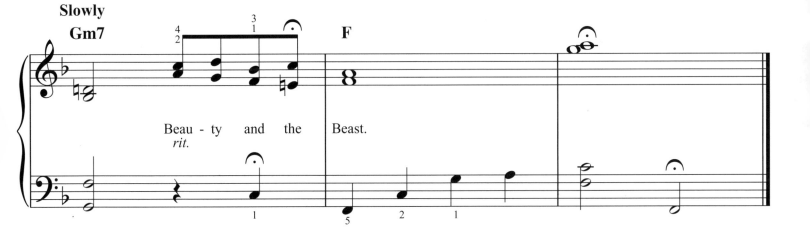

EVERMORE
(As performed by Josh Groban)

Music by ALAN MENKEN
Lyrics by TIM RICE

Moderately slow, with freedom

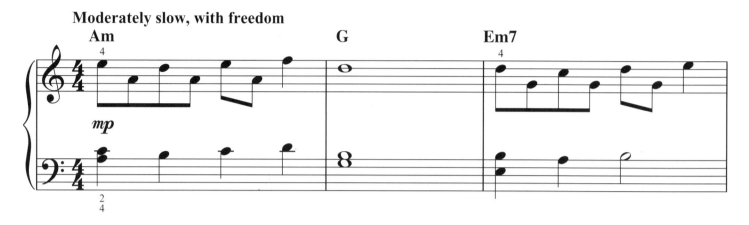

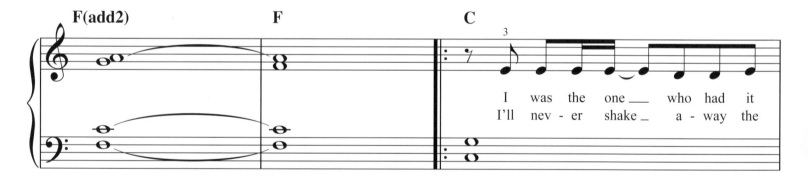

I was the one ___ who had it
I'll nev-er shake ___ a-way the

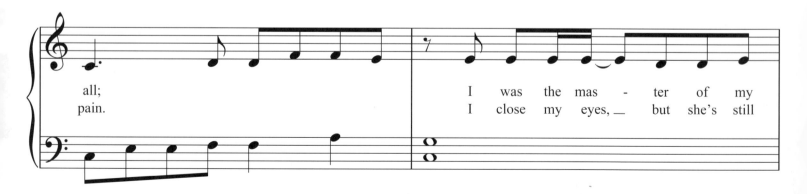

all;
pain.

I was the mas-ter of my
I close my eyes, ___ but she's still

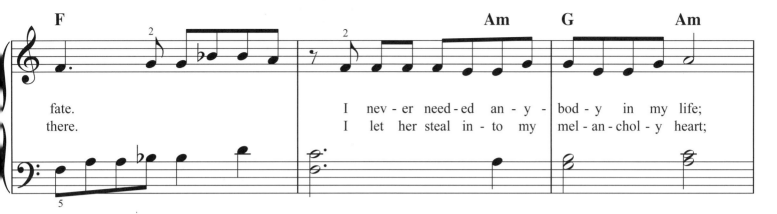

F

fate.
there.

I nev - er need - ed an - y -
I let her steal in - to my

Am   G   Am

bod - y in my life;
mel - an - chol - y heart;

F   C/E

I learned the truth __ too
it's more than I ____ can

1.
Gsus   G

late.

2.
G

bear. _____

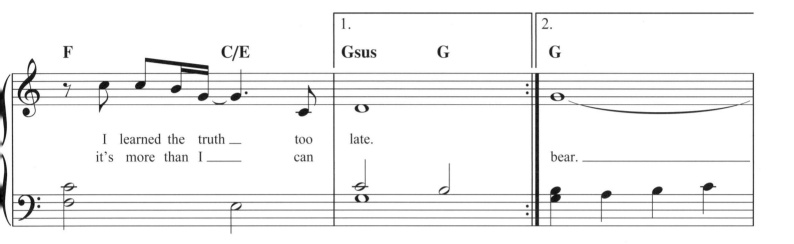

F   G   F   C

____   Now I know she'll nev - er leave me,   e - ven

mf

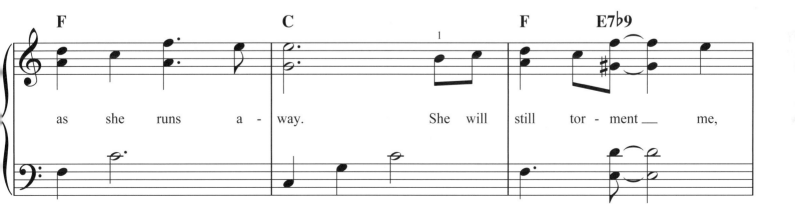

F   C   F   E7♭9

as she runs a - way.   She will still tor - ment __ me,

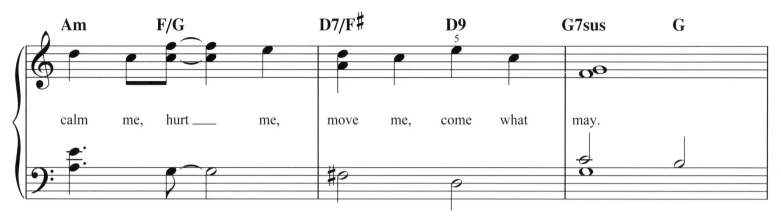

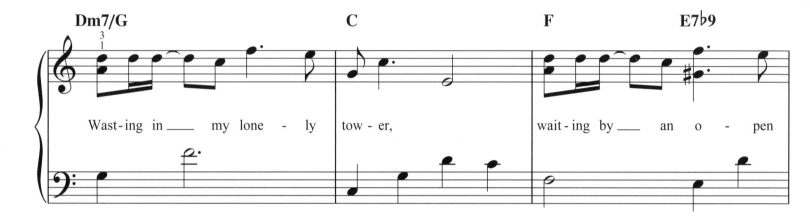

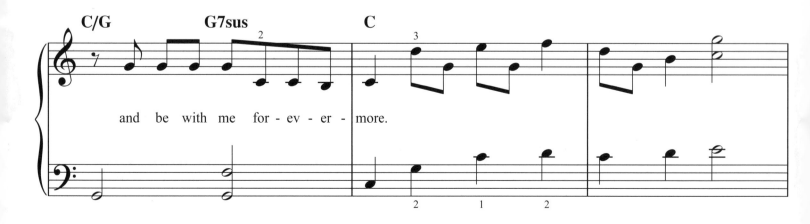

I rage a - gainst __ the trials of love. I curse the fad - ing of the

light. Though she's al - read - y flown so far be - yond my reach,

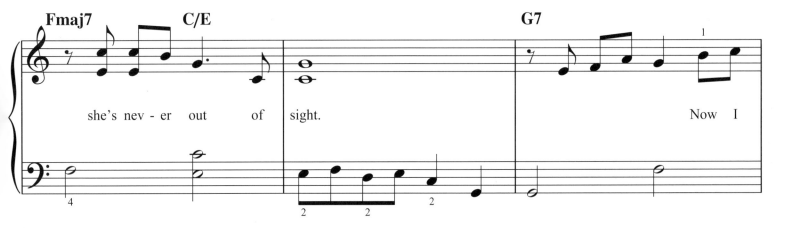

she's nev - er out of sight. Now I

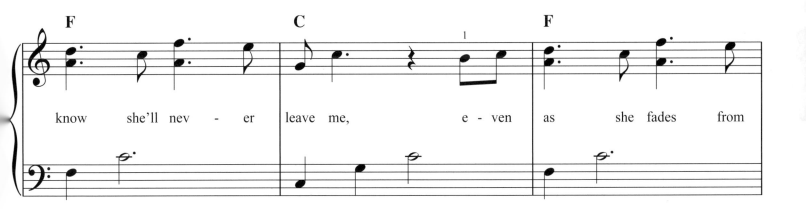

know she'll nev - er leave me, e - ven as she fades from

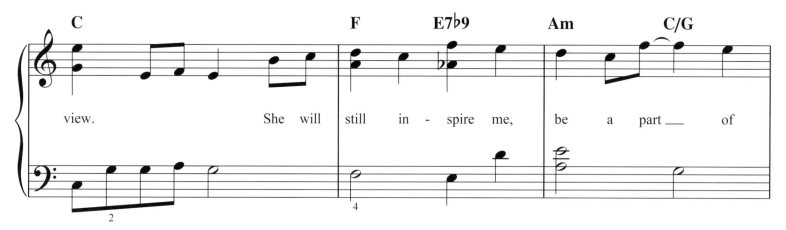

view. She will still in - spire me, be a part ___ of

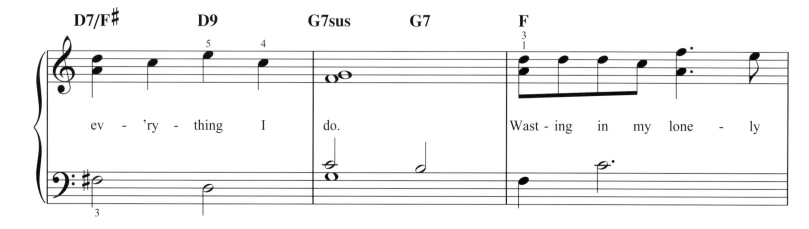

ev - 'ry - thing I do. Wast - ing in my lone - ly

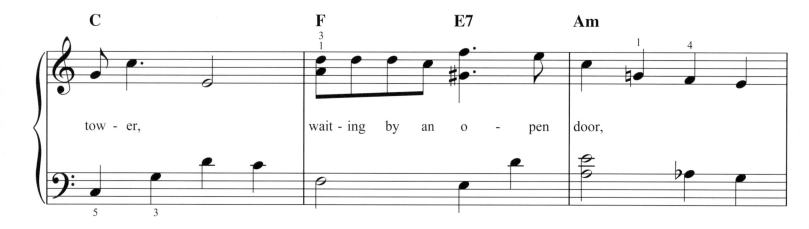

tow - er, wait - ing by an o - pen door,

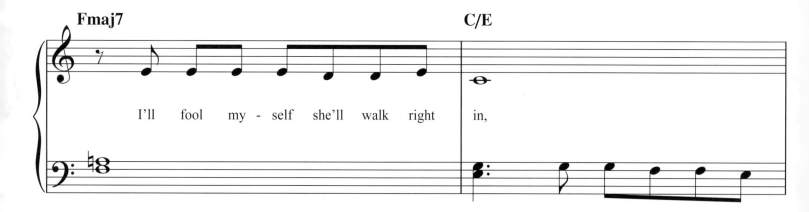

I'll fool my - self she'll walk right in,

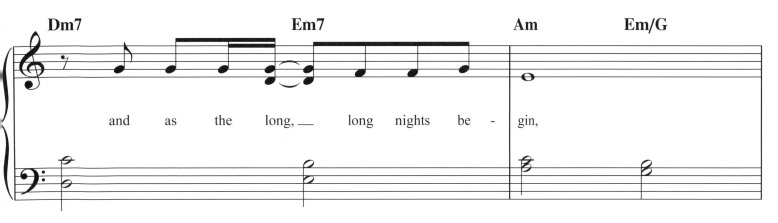

and as the long, __ long nights be - gin,

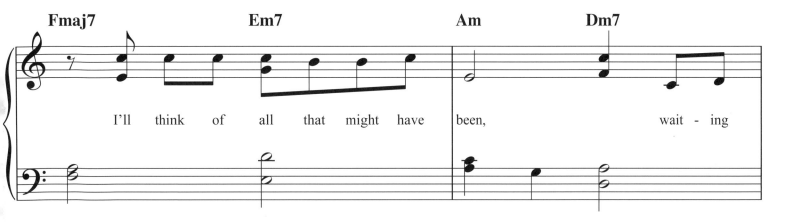

I'll think of all that might have been, waiting

here for ev - er - more.

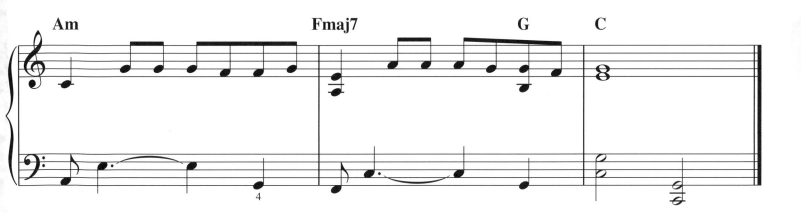